THE SCHOOLS HISTORY PROJECT
S·H·P
OFFICIAL TEXT

**THIS IS HISTORY!**

# King John

## A KEY STAGE 3 INVESTIGATION INTO MEDIEVAL MONARCHY

### DALE BANHAM

### IAN DAWSON

HODDER
EDUCATION
www.hoddereducation.co.uk

## The Schools History Project

Set up in 1972 to bring new life to history for students aged 13–16, the Schools History Project continues to play an innovatory role in secondary history education. From the start, SHP aimed to show how good history has an important contribution to make to the education of a young person. It does this by creating courses and materials which both respect the importance of up-to-date, well-researched history and provide enjoyable learning experiences for students.

Since 1978 the Project has been based at Trinity and All Saints University College Leeds. It continues to support, inspire and challenge teachers through the annual conference, regional courses and website: http://www.schoolshistoryproject.org.uk. The Project is also closely involved with government bodies and awarding bodies in the planning of courses for Key Stage 3, GCSE and A level.

**Note:** The wording and sentence structure of some written sources have been adapted and simplified to make them accessible to all pupils, while faithfully preserving the sense of the original.

Words printed in SMALL CAPITALS are defined in the Glossary on page 66.

© Dale Banham and Ian Dawson 2000

First published in 2000
by Hodder Education,
an Hachette company UK
338 Euston Road
London NW1 3BH

Reprinted 2001, 2003, 2004, 2005, 2006, 2008, 2010, 2011, 2012

Layouts by Amanda Hawkes
Artwork by Art Construction, Richard Duszczak,
Oxford Illustrators, Tony Randell, Steve Smith
Typeset in Goudy by Wearset, Boldon, Tyne and Wear
Printed and bound in Dubai

A catalogue entry for this book is available from the British Library

**ISBN-13: 978 0 719 58539 5**
Teachers' Resource Book ISBN 978 0 7195 8540 1

# ◆ Contents

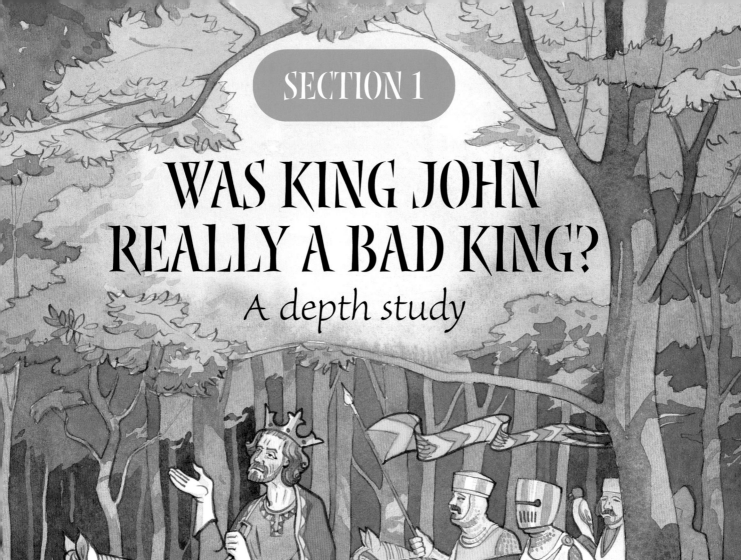

# SECTION 1

# WAS KING JOHN REALLY A BAD KING?

## A depth study

"I am John, King of England. Eight hundred years ago, I ruled England for seventeen of the most important years in our history. I am so famous I'm sure you have heard of me already. But let me warn you, you won't have heard the truth!

Many people say that I was a poor king, who made many mistakes. Some so-called historians have even had the cheek to say that I was the worst king England has ever had. They are wrong!

In my opinion I did a good job, even though my father (Henry II) and brother (Richard the Lionheart) left me with huge problems and very little money. I worked amazingly hard and had great success, but I never get the credit I deserve. People always believe the stories my enemies tell."

"The main reason that people dislike me is because of the Robin Hood legend. In the Robin Hood stories I am always shown as a greedy, cowardly ruler who treated people very unfairly – but do you always believe everything you see and hear? You have to remember that these stories were just written to entertain people. Nobody even knows for certain if Robin Hood existed. So how do you know these stories are telling the truth about me, King John, one of the cleverest men who ever ruled England?

In this book I am going to lead you on an investigation into my exciting life, although someone much less interesting will keep interrupting me to set you some Activities.

History is exciting because you can make up your own mind from the evidence. Do not believe what others have written; find out for yourself. This book will help you decide whether I was really a bad king...although I am sure you are far too clever to believe that!"

**SOURCE 1** This film was made in 1973. In this scene Robin Hood steals all the money King John and the Sheriff of Nottingham have taken from poor people in taxes.

"In order to carry out your investigation you will need to know a little about my loving family. This is my family tree, starting with my father Henry II. Some of my family have been turned into heroes, leaving me as the family villain. It is so unfair!"

"Eleanor of Aquitaine, my beautiful mother, was 30 years old and just divorced from the King of France when she married my father. You can imagine the scandal – Henry was only 19! Their happiness didn't last. She supported my brothers when they rebelled against my father, so he kept her under armed guard for the rest of his reign. He called her his 'hated Queen'. Richard and I treated her a lot better because she helped us control our lands in France. I was very upset when she died in 1204."

"Henry II is my father. He was hard-working, made the barons obey the laws and increased the size of his empire. He ruled over land from Scotland to Spain, as you can see from the map on page 7. I was his favourite son, of course."

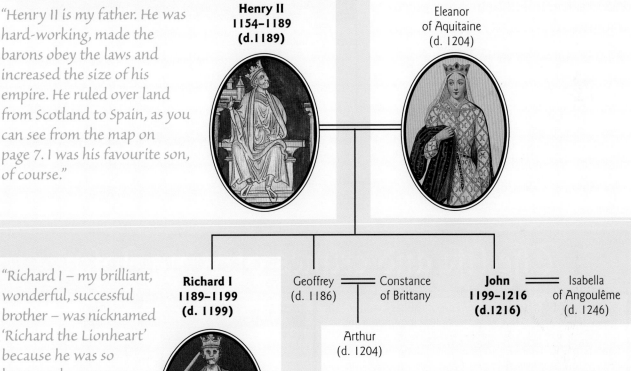

**Henry II
1154–1189
(d.1189)**

Eleanor
of Aquitaine
(d. 1204)

"Richard I – my brilliant, wonderful, successful brother – was nicknamed 'Richard the Lionheart' because he was so brave and courageous in battle. How I hated him! Everyone thinks Richard was a hero, just because he fought in the CRUSADES (though he never did win back Jerusalem) and defeated the French king. People forget that huge taxes had to be paid to fund his Crusades. And, he left me to do all the hard work, to run the country, while he was away on his adventures."

**Richard I
1189–1199
(d. 1199)**

Geoffrey
(d. 1186)

Constance
of Brittany

**John
1199–1216
(d.1216)**

Isabella
of Angoulême
(d. 1246)

Arthur
(d. 1204)

"Arthur is my nephew. When Richard died, Arthur thought he should be king. He joined forces with the King of France and tried to steal my crown. I put him in prison, where he died. People often feel sorry for Arthur, but he was a traitor; and traitors deserve to die, however young they are."

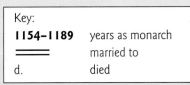

Key:
**1154–1189** years as monarch
━━━ married to
d. died

**SOURCE 2** John's family tree.

You have met King John and heard his opinions. He clearly thinks he was a success, even if most people disagree with him. Now it is time for you to begin your own investigation of the man who has been called 'the worst king who ever sat on the English throne'. Here is a summary of John's story, as it usually appears in the Robin Hood tales. It will help you understand:

◆ the main events in John's life
◆ what John is supposed to have done so badly.

Some of the key events take place overseas. Make sure you refer to the map on page 7 as you read the story.

## ACTIVITY

1 Design a graph like the one below to record the main events in John's life. The graph should show when things went well for John and when things went badly. Imagine John in a hot air balloon. The balloon rises when John is successful and drops when he is in trouble.

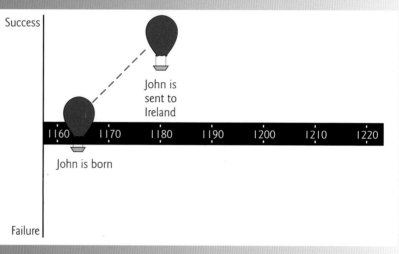

2 Make a list of all the reasons why John was 'a bad king'. Divide your list into two sections:
a) the people he quarrelled with
b) his personality and the things he was not good at.

# The life and crimes of King John

**Lackland** John was born on Christmas Eve, 1167. In 1185, King Henry sent John to rule Ireland. But, this plan failed: John and his young friends insulted important Irish barons by giggling at their long beards, and the Irish barons soon rebelled against him. With no land to rule, John was nicknamed 'Lackland'.

EMPIRE OF HENRY II

**John breaks his father's heart**

Rebels
John

My favourite son!

In 1189, John secretly joined Richard and King Philip II of France in a rebellion against his father. When Henry was shown a list of the rebels he was shocked to find John's name on it. He never recovered from John's betrayal, and died soon afterwards from a broken heart.

## John plots against his brother

Richard was crowned king in 1189. He gave John land and money, but that did not stop John plotting against him. John and King Philip II of France tried to take control of Richard's land while he was away on Crusade. When Richard was captured on his way home from the Holy Land, John did nothing to help.

## Richard returns

Don't be afraid, John. You're still young. You've got into bad company and it is those who have led you astray that I will punish.

In 1194, Richard was released from prison on payment of a huge ransom. He regained the land that King Philip II of France had taken from him, and John was forced to ask for his brother's forgiveness. Richard did not punish John.

In 1199, Richard was fatally wounded fighting in France and named John as his heir.

## A rival for the throne

After Richard's death, John's claim to the throne was supported by the barons of England and Normandy. However, the barons in the rest of the empire chose John's twelve year old nephew, Arthur of Brittany, as their ruler. In 1202, John captured Arthur and put him in prison. Arthur was never seen again. Many people believed that Arthur had been murdered. One source claims that, in a drunken rage, John killed Arthur, tied him to a heavy stone and threw him in the River Seine.

## Soft-sword

In 1200, John divorced his wife and married a rich French girl called Isabella, who was only 12 years old. This caused problems because Isabella had been promised to the French baron Hugh of Lusignan. Hugh complained to King Philip II of France, so Philip invaded John's land in France. Most of John's French barons happily welcomed Philip. By 1205, John had lost most of his land in France. These defeats earned John the new nickname. . .'Soft-sword'.

## Ruling England

That sounds interesting. I must pop down and watch when I've finished counting my money.

John was determined to regain the land he had lost in France. He made the English people pay huge taxes to fund a strong army. He fined people heavily and put them in prison when they could not pay their debts. John used his courts to help his friends, and to punish anyone he did not like. He was a cruel king, who liked nothing better than to see prisoners tortured in dirty dungeons.

AARGH!

### John quarrels with the Pope

In 1205, John quarrelled with the Pope. They disagreed over who should be the new ARCHBISHOP OF CANTERBURY. John refused to let Stephen Langton, the Pope's choice, enter the country. In 1208, the Pope punished John by passing an INTERDICT over England and Wales. This meant that church services stopped and no marriages or burials could take place. John retaliated by taking away all the Church's property and punishing many monks. In 1209, the Pope EXCOMMUNICATED John. This meant that he would go to hell when he died. Eventually, in 1213, John gave in to the Pope.

### John quarrels with France – again

In 1214, John attacked France. His army was crushed by King Philip II of France at the battle of Bouvines. John's hopes of regaining his land in France were destroyed. All his money and all those taxes had been wasted.

Failure! Failure!

### The barons rebel

John's defeat in France angered many barons. If he had won, they might have forgiven him for the way he ruled England, but now they rebelled. In May 1215 the rebel barons captured London and forced John to agree to a set of rules about how to govern the country. These rules were written down in a charter, known as Magna Carta.

Demands

Failure! Failure!

### The end of John

John did not change his ways after Magna Carta. He broke the agreement, so the barons invited Prince Louis of France to take over as king. During the war against Louis, John lost many of the crown jewels when his baggage train sank in the quicksands of the Wash. Shortly afterwards, in 1216, he died at Newark. It is thought that John died from dysentery (fever with serious diarrhoea) after eating too many peaches and drinking too much beer!

The position in 1216.

By the end of his reign, John had lost much of his father's empire. The map opposite shows you how disastrous his reign had been . . .

SOURCE 3 A map of the Angevin Empire ruled over by Henry II.

# ◆ First impressions of King John

You have now read the story that King John was complaining about on page 2. It does seem that John was a very bad king. This page gives you the chance to pull together the criticisms about John that have been made so far. But it also does something else that is equally important.

This book isn't just helping you learn about John and about kings in the Middle Ages. It will also help you to answer written questions and write better essays. If you sneak a look at pages 38–39 you'll see how you'll do this with the help of a Grand Prix track!

Stage 3: **THE BAD KING STRAIGHT**
a) Explain why many people think that John was a bad king.
b) Give examples of the bad things John is supposed to have done.

The History Grand Prix will help you plan your essay on King John, but it's not a good idea to leave all the hard work until the very end. This page helps you get started by writing a draft of the paragraph for the Bad King Straight. Writing a draft is very important, even if it does sound like a tedious chore. No writer, even a famous author, expects the words to come out exactly right first time. It's just like anything else: the more you practise playing a particular piece of music or taking corner kicks, the better you'll get.

So, always draft a paragraph. Then re-read it: does it make sense? Have you missed out an important piece of evidence? Have you made any spelling mistakes? Correcting your first draft is one of the tricks that can improve your work.

## ACTIVITY

Write a paragraph in which you try to prove that John was a bad king. Use the hamburger approach (see opposite) to help you write a good paragraph. And remember, your argument should be supported with evidence from pages 4–7.

To cheer you up you should know that it's taken me an hour so far to write this page, and I've only done two drafts!

# ◆ What makes a good paragraph?

A good paragraph, just like a good medieval monarch, needs certain qualities:

- ◆ **Step 1:** It should start with an opening statement. This statement outlines the **argument** of the paragraph and **links** the paragraph to the **question**.
- ◆ **Step 2:** The opening statement is followed by evidence. It is very important that you provide **evidence** to support your **argument**. Why should people believe your argument if you haven't got any evidence to back it up? The more evidence you use, the stronger your argument becomes.
- ◆ **Step 3:** It finishes with a concluding statement. This statement gives your **answer** to the **question** you have been asked, and it links the evidence to the question. If you include evidence but do not use a concluding statement to link it to the question, the evidence is pointless.

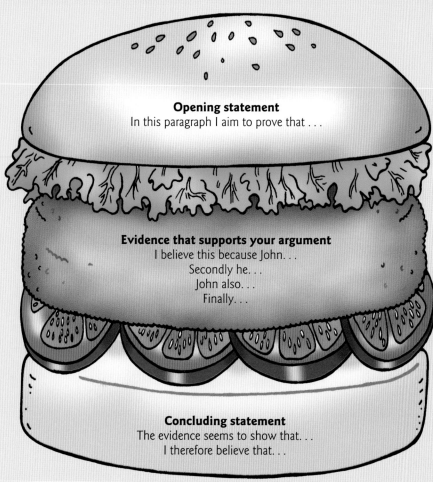

**Opening statement**
In this paragraph I aim to prove that . . .

**Evidence that supports your argument**
I believe this because John. . .
Secondly he. . .
John also. . .
Finally. . .

**Concluding statement**
The evidence seems to show that. . .
I therefore believe that. . .

A good paragraph is like a good hamburger. The opening and concluding statements are the buns which hold the burger together. The evidence is the meat which comes between the buns. Just as all the parts of a hamburger are important for a balanced meal, all the parts of the paragraph are important, too.

- ◆ If you forget the meat (the evidence), or there isn't much of it, the meal is tasteless.
- ◆ If you forget the bottom bun (the concluding statement) the meat/evidence falls out.

**You can use the sentence starters already given to help you, or you can invent your own.**

## ◆ What does the evidence say about John?

*"So now you know why people say I was 'a really bad king'. I hope you're too clever to fall for that story though. I expect you're already asking questions like:*

◆ *How do we know this story is true?*
◆ *Where's the evidence to support this story?*

*Now you need to use your brain to answer these questions. That story was built up from contemporary sources, which are sources that were written around the time that I lived. They say that I was a terrible king, but you need to work out how truthful they are. Just because they were written at the time the events they talk about took place, doesn't mean they tell the truth."*

## ACTIVITY

1 This table lists John's faults mentioned in the story on pages 4–6. Does the evidence for these faults come from contemporary sources? Complete your copy of this table to find out.

| Fault | Which sources give evidence of this fault? |
|---|---|
| John was cruel | |
| John was greedy for money | |
| John was not religious | |
| John was a poor war leader | |
| other faults (be specific) | |

2 What are your impressions of John from Sources 1–4?
  a) Write down five descriptive words that sum up each writer's view of John.
  b) Choose a piece of music that symbolises their opinion of John.
  c) What do all these writers have in common?
  d) Do you expect them to be truthful? Why?
  e) Can you think of a reason why they might not be truthful, about John in particular?
3 Now look at Source 5.
  a) What is Matthew Paris saying about John?
  b) Does this prove John was a bad king?
  c) What can you learn about Matthew Paris from this source?

> **SOURCE 1** Written by Matthew Paris, a monk from the monastery at St Albans, near London.
>
> *John lost Normandy and many other lands because of his own laziness. He always took money from his people and destroyed their property. He hated his wife and she him. He gave orders that her lovers were to be throttled on her bed. John was jealous of many barons and seduced their daughters and sisters. He was a tyrant.*

**SOURCE 2** Written by Gervase, a monk from Canterbury, in Kent.

*After arguing with the Pope, John ordered the few monks who remained at Canterbury, including the blind and crippled, out of the country. He said that all monks were public enemies. The whole of England was taxed heavily. He imprisoned many, bound them in irons and only released them in return for money.*

**SOURCE 3** Written by Roger of Wendover, a monk from the monastery at St. Albans.

*The King's men dragged priests from their horses and robbed and beat them. The King's judges refused to help the priests. The servants of a sheriff on the Welsh borders came to the royal court with a prisoner who had robbed and murdered a priest. They asked the King what they should do with him. John said, 'He has killed an enemy of mine. Untie him and let him go.'*

*In 1209, a priest called Geoffrey said it was not safe for priests to work for the King any longer. John heard of this and Geoffrey was imprisoned in chains, clad in a cloak of lead and starved. Weakened and crushed, Geoffrey died an agonising death.*

**SOURCE 5** This picture was drawn by Matthew Paris, the monk who wrote Source 1.

**SOURCE 4** Written by a monk from Barnwell, near Cambridge.

*John was a great ruler, but not a happy one. He experienced good and bad times. He stole from his own people. He trusted strangers, but not the people he ruled over. In the end, he was deserted by his own men. Few people mourned when he died.*

John's crown looks as if it is about to fall off his head. This gives the impression that John was not in control of his kingdom.

John's body blocks out much of the church in the background. John was criticised for ignoring the rights of the Church and treating it badly.

John is sitting on a campaign stool, not a throne. This shows that he was always fighting wars and the country was never at peace.

# ◆ *Testing the evidence*

"Historians like you have to be as clever as kings. I would not have been a successful king if I had believed everything people told me. Imagine: if I had believed what people told me about how much money they had, I would never have collected any taxes! You need to think just as carefully about Sources 1–5. Do you believe what they say? They were written by monks but they might not be trustworthy."

SOURCE TESTERS 'R' US

## ACTIVITY

**1** Test Sources 1–5 for reliability:
   **a)** Read the background information on each source.
   **b)** Put each source through the four quality control checks below, and give the source a reliability rating out of 5.
   **c)** Explain your answer. Which quality control checks did the source pass and which did it fail?
   **d)** Present your findings in a table like the one below.

| | Reliability rating | Reasons for rating |
|---|---|---|
| Source 1 – Matthew Paris | | |

**2** Can a source be reliable about some things but not about others? Can you think of an example of this?

**3** Write a hamburger paragraph (see page 9) explaining why the evidence about King John may be unreliable. Make sure you use examples from Sources 1–5 on pages 10–11. And remember, this paragraph is going to be useful later on for the History Grand Prix, so keep it safe.

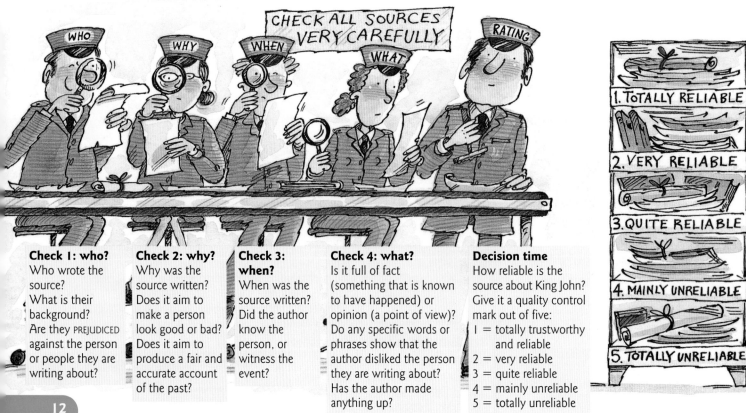

CHECK ALL SOURCES VERY CAREFULLY

WHO   WHY   WHEN   WHAT   RATING

1. TOTALLY RELIABLE
2. VERY RELIABLE
3. QUITE RELIABLE
4. MAINLY UNRELIABLE
5. TOTALLY UNRELIABLE

**Check 1: who?**
Who wrote the source? What is their background? Are they PREJUDICED against the person or people they are writing about?

**Check 2: why?**
Why was the source written? Does it aim to make a person look good or bad? Does it aim to produce a fair and accurate account of the past?

**Check 3: when?**
When was the source written? Did the author know the person, or witness the event?

**Check 4: what?**
Is it full of fact (something that is known to have happened) or opinion (a point of view)? Do any specific words or phrases show that the author disliked the person they are writing about? Has the author made anything up?

**Decision time**
How reliable is the source about King John? Give it a quality control mark out of five:
1 = totally trustworthy and reliable
2 = very reliable
3 = quite reliable
4 = mainly unreliable
5 = totally unreliable

# ◆ *Background information on Sources 1–5*

These sources were all written by monks. Nearly all sources from the Middle Ages were written by monks. Monks were part of the Catholic Church, so the Pope was their leader. King John was very unpopular with the Church because of his long quarrel with the Pope. As a result, most monks did not have anything good to say about John.

**Source 3** was written by Roger of Wendover ten years after John's death. Roger was a monk at St Albans Abbey. He never met John, but thought John was a tyrant, who ruled his people unfairly and cruelly. Most of Roger's work is probably based on gossip. Many barons visited his abbey and told him stories, which he used in his chronicle. His work contains mistakes. Roger describes how John killed a priest called Geoffrey, but records show Geoffrey was alive ten years after John died! Roger also claims that John pardoned a prisoner who had murdered a priest, but records show that John ordered anyone who injured a churchman to be hanged from the nearest oak tree.

**Sources 1 and 5** are by Matthew Paris. Matthew was not even born when John became king, and he never met John. He took over from Roger as the chronicler at St Albans Abbey in 1236 and copied Roger's opinions about John. Some of Matthew's stories are supported by documents, but his descriptions of John are often even further from the truth than Roger's. Matthew and Roger supported the barons against John partly because they hated any type of taxation.

**Source 2** was written by Gervase, a monk at Canterbury Cathedral from 1163–1210. He was well informed about events because many travellers passed through Canterbury on their way to France. Gervase is usually uncritical of the people he writes about.

**Source 4** was written by a monk from Barnwell, near Cambridge, probably between 1220 and 1230. The writer generally wrote about people and events objectively. This means that he did not allow his own personal feelings to influence what he was writing. Even when John fell out with the Church, he says that it was not all John's fault.

*"Didn't I tell you not to believe anything these monks say about me? They're all lying! Are you changing your mind about me yet?"*

## ACTIVITY

Which of these statements do you agree with at this stage of your investigation?
a) John was definitely a poor king.
b) John was probably a poor king.
c) John was possibly a poor king.
d) John was a great king.

*Make sure you don't listen to John too much. It's true that all the sources were written by monks, but can all of them be lying?*

# HE NEVER HAD A CHANCE!

## All about the problems John inherited from his father and his brother

"By now I hope you are very suspicious of that 'bad king' story. Now I'll give you another reason to tear it up. The monks, my enemies, make it seem as if I caused all the problems in England. But, let me tell you, that isn't true. It was my father and brother who created the problems, and I was left to deal with them. They angered the Church. They upset the barons. They left me short of money to defend our land in France. I inherited such terrible problems that I never stood a chance of being a successful king.

You don't believe me? Well, I suppose you shouldn't believe everything I say, even if I was King of England. You need to find out for yourself. In the next part of your investigation you are going to study the problems I faced when I became king.

You are going to write me a report, using the information in this Unit to help you."

## ACTIVITY

It is 1199, and the beginning of John's reign. John wants you to brief him on his problems. You can write your report or record a tape.

Your report should have three sections:

a) What will people expect John to do as king? Does John have the personal qualities needed to carry out these responsibilities?

b) How serious are John's problems? Why are his opponents such a danger to him?

c) Your own honest summary of whether John can succeed. You will be able to use this report later on for the Inheritance Straight of your History Grand Prix, so keep it safe.

Stage 5: **THE INHERITANCE STRAIGHT**
a) Explain the problems that John inherited.
b) Explain how difficult these problems were.

# What did people expect from their king?

A day in the life of SUPER KING!

**A warrior**
The king was in charge of the royal army. He led it into battle. A king who failed in battle was likely to fail as king, because he had to be a brave and successful soldier to win respect.

**A law-maker**
The king made the laws but he had to consult other people. Successful kings listened to their barons then made important decisions by themselves.

**A judge**
The king had to settle disputes and punish people who broke the law. He put people on trial in his own court, or sent judges around the country to settle cases for him. Kings needed to keep law and order. People expected the courts to be fair.

**A protector of the Church**
People believed that the king was God's deputy on earth; that kings were chosen by God to rule over them. They expected the king to protect and respect the Church. Kings had to support, and be fair to, the Church.

**A communicator**
A successful king needed to be hard-working and energetic. He had to travel around the country and keep in touch with his people.

## YOUR REPORT TO JOHN: SECTION A)

1 Work in pairs. Choose two of the roles illustrated in the cartoons and list as many personal qualities as you can think of which might help a king perform those roles successfully. For example, you might think a king needs to be intelligent to be a law-maker.
2 Make a class list.
3 Look at Sources 1–3. Which of the personal qualities do these sources say John had, and which do they say he did not have?
4 Now, write the first part of your report. And remember, you will have to be very tactful if you are going to tell John about his weaknesses.

**SOURCE 1** Richard I talking about John. It was written down by Roger of Howden, who knew Richard, in his chronicle.

*My brother John is not the man to conquer a country. My brother is not the man to win land for himself if there is anyone able to make the slightest resistance to his efforts.*

**SOURCE 2** W.L. Warren, a modern historian, writing in his book *King John* which was published in 1961.

*John was hard-working and very clever. At the same time he was hot tempered and stubborn. He was secretive and suspicious. He was relentless in revenge, cruel and mocking when he had men in his clutches. He could not resist the temptation to kick a man when he was down. John could be tough and in battle he could plan good moves, but he never displayed the courage that inspires an army and he always tended to panic when things were not going his way.*

**SOURCE 3** R.V. Turner, a modern historian, writing in his book *King John* which was published in 1994.

*John was no coward. He was good at planning for war and was a skilled soldier and besieger of castles. John had the potential for success. He was intelligent and good at administration. However, too many personality faults held him back. He was secretive, arrogant and cruel. He lacked the likeable qualities of his brother and father. John was very untrustworthy and was always jealous and suspicious of people. He would not listen to advice. It was very difficult for men to stay loyal to him.*

15

## ◆ **What problems did John face?**

"Being a king was very demanding – you can see that now, can't you? There was none of this lying around being spoilt. The job was more like a long cross-country slog. And, as if it wasn't hard enough already, people put a great many hurdles in your way. You had to jump over, swerve round, or duck under obstacles that could bring you crashing down."

SUCCESS

French Forest

Baron's Brook

Church Challenge

1 Look at the three Secret Service reports on pages 17–19. A report has been compiled for each of John's opponents.
2 Grade each opponent on a scale of 1–5, with 1 as an easy problem to solve and 5 as a problem that John will not be able to overcome.
3 Now, write the second part of your report, explaining which of John's opponents presented him with his biggest problem and why.

# Dangerous opponent

### number 1

**Name:** *Pope Innocent III*

- Born in 1160. Became Pope in 1198.

- Young, intelligent, and very ambitious.

- His main aim is to increase the power of the Pope and reduce the power of Europe's monarchs.

- WARNING: this man will interfere. He has already become involved in disputes in other European countries.

## What is the problem?

The Church in England is part of the Roman Catholic Church, which is run by the Pope, who lives in Rome. The English CLERGY obey the Pope, rather than the English king. The Church owns a great deal of land, and is very rich and powerful. It also has its own courts, which often meddle in matters which are supposed to be dealt with by the royal courts. English kings do not like the way the Pope and the Church interfere in matters of government, and want to find a way to stop them.

## How did Henry II and Richard I tackle the problem?

Thomas Becket was a close friend of Henry II, until Henry appointed him Archbishop of Canterbury. Henry hoped that Becket would reduce the power of the church courts. Many churchmen did not want Becket as Archbishop because they thought that Becket would do as Henry wished. Becket, however, was determined to prove them wrong.

When Henry tried to reduce the power of the church courts, Becket opposed him. Henry was angry and forced Becket to leave the country. In 1170, Henry allowed Becket to return to England. It was not long before Becket began to oppose Henry again. Henry was furious and angrily shouted, 'Will no one rid me of this troublesome priest?' Four knights heard this. In December 1170, they burst into Canterbury Cathedral and murdered Becket. Henry was blamed for Becket's death.

Richard I side-stepped the problem of how to deal with the Church by going on Crusade. The Pope asked him to join the Crusade to the Holy Land in the Middle East. The Holy Land was controlled by Muslims and the Pope wanted it controlled by Christians. Although Richard did not capture Jerusalem his Crusade helped him stay on good terms with the Pope.

Henry II argues with Thomas Becket, the Archbishop of Canterbury.

## Dangerous opponent

**Name:** *Roger Bigod, earl of Norfolk*

- ◆ Son of Hugh Bigod, a powerful baron who rebelled against Henry II.

- ◆ When Hugh died, Henry II punished Roger by forcing him to pay his father's debts and refusing to allow him to take over his father's earldom.

- ◆ In 1189, Richard I let Roger have his earldom and lands in return for 1000 marks, far more than the going rate.

- ◆ One of the most powerful barons in the country. He is very rich and controls two castles.

- ◆ WARNING: this man may rebel – it runs in the family!

### What is the problem?

The barons are the most powerful and wealthy group of people in the country. They supply the king with an army in wartime, and help the king maintain law and order in peacetime. In return they expect a say in how the country is run. If the king angers the barons they may refuse to obey him. They have their own castles and armies and could be a real threat to the king. If a king wants to be successful he must manage the barons very carefully and avoid angering them.

### How did Henry II and Richard I tackle the problem?

Henry II kept strong control over the barons. He destroyed more than 300 of their castles, and built royal castles in areas where he thought the barons were a threat. For example, Henry built Orford Castle on the coast so that he was protected against invasion and could control Hugh Bigod, the most powerful man in East Anglia. Henry also sent judges around the country to hear cases in local courts. This meant that the barons lost control of the local courts. Some leading barons rebelled against Henry in 1173.

Orford Castle in Suffolk.

Richard I also angered the barons. They paid high taxes to fund Richard's Crusade, and even higher taxes to pay his ransom when he was imprisoned on his way home. The barons were then forced to pay out even more money to equip Richard's army and navy for war in France. A chronicler wrote, 'No age can remember, or history tell of, any king who demanded and took so much money from his kingdom.'

Many barons are angry with the way the Angevin Empire has been ruled. They did not dare to rebel against Richard because of his great skill as a soldier, but it will not take much more to push them into rebellion. They feel that their power has been reduced and that they have been forced to pay unreasonable taxes.

## Dangerous opponent

**Name:** *Philip II, King of France*

◆ Born in 1165.
Ruled France since the age of 15.

◆ Determined, intelligent and very cunning – always trying to start arguments between his rivals.

◆ Very rich. He can afford a large army and long wars.

◆ His main aim is to destroy the Angevin Empire.

◆ WARNING: this man cannot be trusted. He will try to take your lands.

### What is the problem?

The Angevin Empire, ruled by Henry II and now by John, includes large parts of France. King Philip of France wants to win back the English lands in France, and has stirred up rebellions which he hopes will weaken England's control over the land. English kings have been forced to fight expensive wars to defend their empire.

It is also difficult for English kings to control their huge empire because travel is very slow. It is only possible to cover about 50 km per day travelling on horseback, so the king has to be constantly on the move to keep in touch with what is happening.

### How did Richard I tackle the problem?

Richard set off on Crusade with Philip, but the two kings fell out when Richard refused to marry Philip's sister. Philip angrily returned to France and invaded Richard's lands in Normandy. He also encouraged John to stir up trouble in England. When Richard returned from the Holy Land, he slowly won back his land in France. He also strengthened his empire's defences by building castles, such as Chateau Gaillard in Normandy. Richard had beaten a stronger opponent, but then Richard was a military genius. He is a very hard act for King John to follow.

Richard on horseback.

### YOUR REPORT TO JOHN: SECTION C)

1 Look at what you have already written for sections **a)** and **b)** of your report. This will help you with section **c)**.

2 Using a scale of 1–5, with 1 as a helpful inheritance and 5 as a very difficult inheritance, decide whether or not John's inherited problems will stop him being a successful king.

3 Now, write a summary paragraph about John's overall chance of success. This is the third part of your report.

## ACTIVITY

John is on trial.

**a)** As you work through the four Investigations in this Unit your task is to gather evidence for the trial. To do this you will use a sorting frame.

**b)** At the end of the Unit, you will use the evidence you have collected to prepare a speech for either the defence or the prosecution.

If you decide that John **was** a failure as king then you will be a lawyer for the prosecution, and your speech will try to prove that John was guilty.

If you decide that John **was not** a failure, you will be a defence lawyer. Your aim will be to prove John not guilty.

And, as a bonus – it's only fair to warn you – you'll be able to use your speech as part of your Grand Prix essay, when you get to John's Reign Chicane!

John, King of England, you are charged with being a failure as king because you:
- foolishly quarrelled with the Pope
- lost your land in France
- caused the barons to rebel
- had very few successes.

To help you organise your research in a way that will eventually help you write a brilliant speech it is a good idea to design a **sorting frame**.

Take three pieces of paper and write down the following headings:

**Sheet 1: Evidence that John was a bad king**
It is a good idea to divide this sheet into two sections:
**a) Evidence that he made mistakes**
**b) Evidence that he was cruel and unfair**

**Sheet 2: Evidence that John was unlucky or that other people let him down**

**Sheet 3: Evidence that John was a good king**
It is also a good idea to divide this sheet into two sections:
**a) Evidence that he was successful and made intelligent decisions**
**b) Evidence that he was hardworking and kind**

As you read through pages 21–28, use these three headings to record any information that you think might help you write your speech later. If you sort your research into categories as you go along you will save time when you come to write your speech, because you won't have to go through your notes and sort them into order.

# ◆ *Investigation one: what did John do well?*

## INVESTIGATION ONE

John doing things well – this may be a new idea to you! But, you shouldn't find it too hard to transfer the information contained in this Investigation onto the good king sheet of your sorting frame. Just don't forget that you have to decide whether it fits into part **a)** or part **b)**.

John was very interested in the royal court. He often sat as judge and decided cases himself. John also travelled around the whole country. He knew England better than previous kings and was hard-working.

John increased the strength of his navy. Richard I had built up a navy and given it a base at Portsmouth, but many of his ships had been destroyed in the wars against France. John built new ships, strengthened Portsmouth's defences, and established a new port at Liverpool.

John carried a small library with him wherever he went. Books were very rare in his time. In 1205, he asked Reginald of Cornhill to send him a history of England.

On feast days John often made arrangements to feed hundreds of PAUPERS. In 1209, 100 paupers were fed in Newcastle. Other kings had done this, but few were as generous as John. Sometimes he would provide meals for as many as 1000 paupers at one sitting.

## ◆ Investigation two: was John foolish to quarrel with the Pope?

You have seen this drawing before on page 6. The caption reminds you about what happened when John quarrelled with the Church. Your task is to put the statements in the boxes into the right categories in your sorting frame.

John chose the new archbishop because it showed that the king, not the Pope, had the most power in England. English kings had always chosen the English bishops.

John made a small fortune by taking the Church's land and property during the Interdict. He was able to use this to finance his wars.

**John quarrels with the Pope** In 1205, John quarrelled with the Pope. They disagreed over who should be the new ARCHBISHOP OF CANTERBURY. John refused to let Stephen Langton, the Pope's choice, enter the country. In 1208, the Pope punished John by passing an INTERDICT over England and Wales. This meant that church services stopped and no marriages or burials could take place. John retaliated by taking away all the Church's property and punishing many monks. In 1209, the Pope EXCOMMUNICATED John. This meant that he would go to hell when he died. Eventually, in 1213, John gave in to the Pope.

A new Pope had been elected in 1198, just before John became king. The new Pope was determined to increase his power. He was a tougher opponent than earlier Popes.

By making peace, John gained the Pope as a powerful ally. The Pope supported John against Philip II of France, and the barons, and he later said that John did not have to keep to Magna Carta.

# ◆ *Investigation three: was John to blame for the loss of his land in France?*

## INVESTIGATION THREE

This is the cartoon you saw on page 5. But does it tell the full truth? You can now learn a little more about John's wars in France, and build up more evidence for the trial. As you read pages 23–24, pick out events and other information about John for your sorting frame. And remember, some should go onto the bad king sheet, some onto the unlucky sheet, and some onto the good king sheet.

Soft-sword

In 1200, John divorced his wife and married a rich French girl called Isabella, who was only 12 years old. This caused problems because Isabella had been promised to the French baron Hugh of Lusignan. Hugh complained to King Philip II of France, so Philip invaded John's land in France. Most of John's French barons happily welcomed Philip. By 1205, John had lost most of his land in France. These defeats earned John the new nickname. . .'Soft-sword'.

## 1. John wins an empire

Although Richard I named John as his heir, John had a rival. His nephew, Arthur of Brittany, thought that he should be king and he was supported by Philip II, the King of France. John had to fight for his crown – and he won! Moving quickly, his army beat both Philip and Arthur. John's reign had got off to an excellent start.

## 2. Rescue at Mirebeau

Peace did not last long. In 1200, John made a mistake. He left his first wife to marry Isabella of Angoulême. Isabella had been about to marry Hugh of Lusignan. Hugh was outraged. He claimed that John had stolen his bride and complained to Philip II. This was the chance Philip had been waiting for. Philip, Hugh and Arthur attacked John's land in France, including Mirebeau Castle where John's mother, Eleanor, was living. John set out immediately. Marching at top speed he and his army covered 80 miles in just two days.

Ralph of Coggeshall, writing in the thirteenth century, tells us what happened next.

*Arthur's army had entered Mirebeau and had closed up all the gates except one. With his army of skilled knights Arthur was confident of victory, but John arrived sooner than he expected. John fought his way into the city, caught all his enemies and freed his mother.*

## 3. Defeat in Normandy

John's success did not last. In 1203, rumours spread that John had murdered Arthur. This caused a rebellion in Brittany and other parts of his empire. Powerful French barons deserted John, and began to support Philip. This made it almost impossible for John to stop Philip taking control of his land in France. To make things worse, John could not even trust his English barons: two of them surrendered one of his French castles without a single arrow being fired. Even Philip thought they were cowardly traitors! John lost Normandy in 1204. After that it was one disaster after another, and Philip's army captured the rest of John's land in France.

# 4. Fighting back

John was soon planning to win back his empire. He skilfully captured Gascony, but when he attacked Anjou his barons let him down again. Without their men, John had to agree to a truce. Philip was too powerful. John had failed to win back his land in France.

John agrees to a truce with Philip II. The truce was sealed with a kiss of peace.

# 5. Bouvines – the last chance

In 1214, John attacked Philip from the south, whilst his allies from Flanders and Germany attacked Philip from the north. His plan worked. He won back some of the land that Philip had taken from him. Then disaster struck. His allies met Philip's army at the battle of Bouvines. If his allies won, John would become the most powerful ruler in Europe. And, at one stage in the battle they were winning: Philip was knocked off his horse and soldiers stabbed at him. Unfortunately for John, however, Philip's bodyguards gathered round him. Philip was saved. The battle then began to go Philip's way. He had a larger army and had organised his troops very carefully. He won, and John was forced to agree to a truce. John had failed in France for the last time.

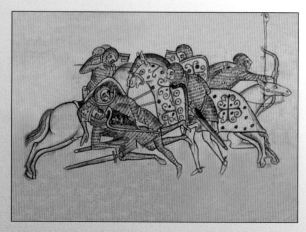

The battle of Bouvines. King Philip has been knocked off his horse and needs to be saved by one of his knights.

# ◆ Investigation four: did John cause the conflict between king and barons?

If a king wanted a peaceful kingdom he had to keep the barons on his side. One reason John was not able to do this was because he was always short of money.

◆ The wars of Henry II and Richard I left John short of money.

◆ John's main aim was to regain his land in France. To do this he needed a large, well-equipped army. He needed foreign mercenaries (soldiers who are paid to fight for a foreign country) to increase the size of his army.

◆ John had to pay for castles to be built and repaired.

◆ The costs of warfare were increasing e.g. soldiers had to be paid higher wages.

Lack of money was a major cause of the rebellion against John, which took place in 1215.

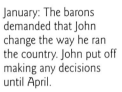

**INVESTIGATION FOUR**

Use this page and pages 26–28 to add information to your sorting frame.

a) Start with the information on the left. Can you find examples of John being unlucky?

b) Use the timeline below. Can you find examples of John making mistakes or bad decisions?

c) Now look at the barons' meeting on the next two pages. Can you find examples of John being cruel and unfair?

## The road to Magna Carta

1205

1212

1213

1214

1215

Some barons refused to help John regain his land in France. John abandoned his plans to invade France, but demanded taxes anyway. This angered the barons because they usually only paid taxes in wartime.

John called off his invasion of Wales because some barons threatened to rebel. John demanded hostages from these barons to make sure they did not plot against him again.

Barons from the north of England refused to help John attack Philip II of France. John marched north to punish them, but the Archbishop of Canterbury threatened to excommunicate his soldiers if he didn't turn back. John turned back.

John demanded taxes from the barons even though his armies had been beaten in France. There was a lot of protest. After John's failure in France some barons were willing to risk rebellion.

January: The barons demanded that John change the way he ran the country. John put off making any decisions until April.

April: The barons arrived at their meeting armed, but John failed to turn up. He had no intention of giving up any of his rights.

May: Rebellion! The barons took control of London.

June: John decided he could not beat the rebel barons. He met them at Runnymede, near Windsor Castle, and agreed to change the way he ran the country. The agreement was written down in Magna Carta (the Great Charter).

# Why did John anger the barons?

If John agrees to what we ask how can we make him keep his word? Can we force him to keep his word when he has all these foreign mercenaries to use against us?

John insults the Church, and he punished churchmen because of his quarrel with the Pope. The king should treat the Church fairly.

Why should we fight in France? My lands in the north of England are a long way from France. I will not gain anything from a war against France. The king wastes money on these pointless wars – which he always loses.

John is far too hard on us. He takes our land if we do not obey his commands. He even takes our sons as hostages, in case we rebel against him. Look at what happened to the sons of those Welsh barons in 1211. John took 28 as hostages and they were all executed, on John's orders, because he thought their fathers had plotted against him.

I do not trust John. I want a say in how our country is run, but he never asks us for advice. He spends all his time with his favourites. John will only work with people like Gerard d'Athee from France. John has put him in charge of the castles at Gloucester, Bristol and Hereford. John lets him punish anyone who steps out of line.

John keeps demanding the scutage tax from us. In the past we paid this 'shield money' instead of sending knights to join the king's army in wartime. But John makes us pay scutage even when he is not going to war – and he is demanding twice what we paid Richard.

I know we have to pay the king when we inherit family land, but John demanded over £6000 from me. I only make £550 a year from the land. £100 would be a fairer price.

John is also squeezing money out of elderly women. When my father died, my mother had to pay John over £3000 so that he wouldn't force her to marry again. She really did not want to remarry so she had no choice but to pay the fine.

John uses the law to punish his enemies and help his friends. If John is against you he will not allow your case to be heard in court. I owed him money when I was Sheriff of Lincolnshire and I couldn't keep up the repayments. John imprisoned me in Rochester Castle. He said I would stay there until I paid every last penny I owed.

## ACTIVITY

1 Using pages 26–27, list all the reasons why the barons were unhappy with the way John ruled the country.
2 Use your list to draw up a charter which gives the king clear rules about how he should govern the country. Your Magna Carta must make sure that the king rules the country fairly and wins the support of the barons.

## Magna Carta

Magna Carta was a set of rules about how the king should treat the FREEMEN of England. PEASANTS were not freemen, so Magna Carta did not protect their rights. Knights, merchants and bishops – as well as barons – were freemen. The barons included these other groups in Magna Carta in order to gain more support. Magna Carta had 63 clauses. They cover a wide range of topics. The most important are listed below.

**Clause 1**   The English Church shall be free. The king must not interfere with the Church.

**Clause 2**   When a baron inherits land he should not have to pay more than £100 to the king.

**Clause 8**   No widow shall be forced to marry as long as she wishes to live without a husband.

**Clause 12**   The king must not demand scutage payments or other taxes without the agreement of the bishops and the barons.

**Clause 21**   Barons should only be fined after a proper trial. The fine should match the crime.

**Clause 39**   No freeman should be arrested, imprisoned, or in any way destroyed without a fair trial.

**Clause 49**   The king will return all hostages given to him by barons.

**Clause 50**   The king will entirely remove the relations of Gerard d'Athee from their jobs.

**Clause 51**   As soon as peace is restored, all foreign mercenaries should leave the country.

**Clause 61**   The barons shall choose 25 barons to make certain that the king keeps this charter. If the king or any of his servants breaks this charter, the 25 barons can take action to make him keep the charter. This includes seizing the king's castles and lands but they cannot attack the king himself, his queen or his children.

# ◆ *Tips for successful speech writing*

Once you have decided whether you will speak for the defence or the prosecution, it is time to write your speech. Here are some important tips to help you.

## Tip 1: select

You will not write a good speech if you simply write down everything there is to know about John. Always keep the research question at the front of your mind, and select the **relevant information**. Information is only relevant if it helps you answer your research question. For example, if you are writing a speech for the prosecution only one of the following statements is relevant. Why?

- ◆ John was born in Oxford on Christmas Eve 1167.
- ◆ He was only 1.65 metres tall.
- ◆ By 1205, John had lost two thirds of the Angevin Empire.

## Tip 2: support

Support all your arguments with evidence. Give at least one example to support each of your main arguments.

## Tip 3: organise

You have already used the hamburger frame to write a good paragraph (see page 9). You now need to go one step further, and organise your speech using the **double hamburger**.

The difference is in the middle. Good lawyers need to do more than provide evidence to support their arguments. They also need to destroy the opposition's argument. You can do this by pointing out the weaknesses in their case and by challenging the reliability of their evidence.

Use the double hamburger framework to help you structure your speech. You can use the sentence starters already given, or you can write your own.

## Tip 4: prepare

Prepare thoroughly before you read out your speech. Underline or highlight the key points you want to make. When you read out your speech, pause before and after these points.

## Tip 5: present

Think carefully about the way you present your speech: look at your audience as much as possible, do not rush, and make sure your audience can understand what you are saying.

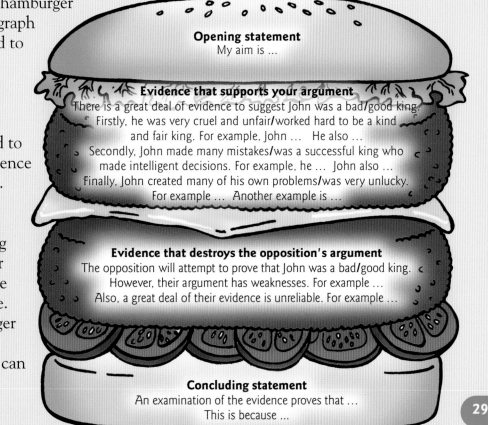

**Opening statement**
My aim is ...

**Evidence that supports your argument**
There is a great deal of evidence to suggest John was a bad/good king. Firstly, he was very cruel and unfair/worked hard to be a kind and fair king. For example, John ...   He also ...
Secondly, John made many mistakes/was a successful king who made intelligent decisions. For example, he ...   John also ...
Finally, John created many of his own problems/was very unlucky.
For example ...   Another example is ...

**Evidence that destroys the opposition's argument**
The opposition will attempt to prove that John was a bad/good king. However, their argument has weaknesses. For example ...
Also, a great deal of their evidence is unreliable. For example ...

**Concluding statement**
An examination of the evidence proves that ...
This is because ...

It's time to fasten your seat belt for the High Speed Historiography Hairpin! If you have seen the History Grand Prix then you know that this Unit will be tough; but I can promise you it will be interesting as well. Are you feeling brave enough for the challenge?

Medieval chroniclers thought John was a tyrant, but historians have changed their interpretations of him since then. You are going to investigate historians' changing ideas and, more interestingly, why they have changed their ideas. That's what historiography is – studying why historians have different ideas about a subject. As you'll find out, historians' ideas are affected by the beliefs and events of their own time.

## ACTIVITY

Look carefully at the information to work out whether John was:
**a)** a hero or a villain to the Tudors
**b)** a hero or a villain to the Victorians.
Use the Key Questions below if you need help, and don't forget to explain your answer.

| Key Question | Tudors | Victorians |
|---|---|---|
| **1** Would they have approved of John's quarrel with the Church? | | |
| **2** Would they have approved of John chasing after the wives and daughters of barons? | | |
| **3** Would they have had sympathy for John when he lost his land in France? | | |
| **4** John rarely asked the barons for advice. He thought that the king should make all the important decisions. Would they have thought that this was the right way to run the country? | | |

**T U D O R S**

The people who lived in England in Tudor times respected strong monarchs like Henry VIII. They expected their monarch to make the important decisions. They did not think Magna Carta was a very significant document. William Shakespeare did not even mention it in his play about King John.

Henry VIII quarrelled with the Pope. He wanted to leave his first wife, Catherine of Aragon, and marry Anne Boleyn. The Pope blocked his plans. In 1534, Henry took the Pope's place as head of the English Church. In retaliation, the Pope excommunicated Henry from the Catholic Church.

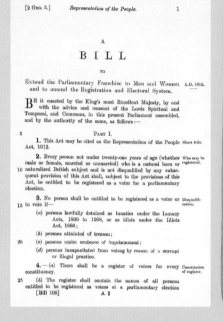

VICTORIA QUEEN OF GREAT BRITAIN
EMPRESS OF INDIA
1837—JUBILEE—1887

During the Victorian period, the country became more democratic, as many more men were given the right to vote. The Victorians thought Magna Carta was very important. They saw it as the beginning of DEMOCRACY.

Queen Victoria ruled over a large empire. This was very important to the people of Britain as it helped them become wealthy. They admired past kings who had increased the size of the empire and who had been successful soldiers.

Many Victorians were regular church-goers and spent lots of money on church buildings. Religion was a very important part of their lives. They also had very strict moral standards. They liked their leaders to be good family men. The Victorians had a clear sense of right and wrong. Law and order was very important to them.

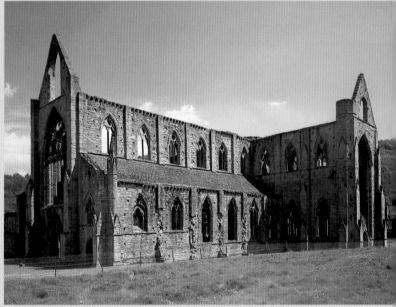

The Tudors were often threatened by foreign invasions. Henry VIII feared attacks from France and Spain. He built castles on the coast to protect the country. England was also in danger during the reign of Elizabeth I. In 1588, the King of Spain, supported by the Pope, sent the Armada to invade England and return the country to Catholicism.

From 1536 to 1539, Henry closed down many monasteries. The enormous wealth of the Church was transferred to the Crown. Henry took control of Church property and land. He made a great deal of money by selling it off to his nobles.

## ACTIVITY

Study pages 32–33.

1 Draw a graph like the one below and complete it to show how interpretations of John have changed since the medieval period.

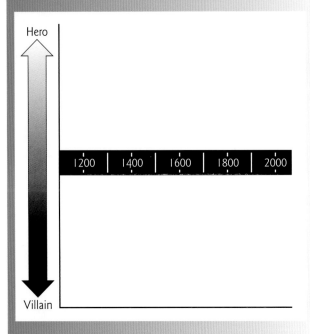

2 Give two reasons why interpretations of John have changed so much.

3 Why do you think that historians still disagree about what John was like?

## How have historians viewed King John?

### Tudor (1485–1603)

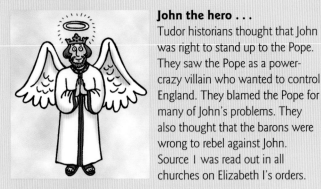

**John the hero . . .**
Tudor historians thought that John was right to stand up to the Pope. They saw the Pope as a power-crazy villain who wanted to control England. They blamed the Pope for many of John's problems. They also thought that the barons were wrong to rebel against John. Source 1 was read out in all churches on Elizabeth I's orders.

### Victorian (1837–1901)

**John the villain . . .**
Victorian historians saw John as a failure and a villain. They thought he created his own problems and was a cruel and wicked king; the Devil in disguise.

### 1950s and 1960s

**John the good . . .**
From 1950, some historians began to challenge the traditional interpretations of John. They were more sympathetic, saying he worked hard. A few even claimed he was an administrative genius, who ran the country as well as anyone could have done. These historians also argued that John was very unlucky. He was up against a powerful Pope and a skilful King of France, who had far more money than him. They also said that John inherited problems from his father and brother.

### Modern historians (1980s and 1990s)

**John the not so good . . .**
Modern historians have mixed views about John. Most accept that he did have some good qualities. However, they argue that historians in the 1950s and 1960s made too much of his skills. They agree that John faced many problems, but say that his actions often made these problems far worse. John had serious faults in his personality that got him into trouble.

## Why have historians viewed John in this way?

**SOURCE 1** An extract from *Homily Against Disobedience and Wilful Religion*, 1571.

*What a disgrace and a shame that the barons rebelled against King John and did not give him help in his lawful wars.*

◆ People in Tudor times saw John as an earlier version of Henry VIII. Both kings quarrelled with the Pope, and both kings stood up to the Pope.
◆ They also admired firm, strict kings who took a leading role in running the country. They believed that rebellions harmed everyone in the country.

**SOURCE 2** An extract from *Short History of the English People*, written by J.R. Green in 1875. This book was a bestseller and was translated into many different languages.

*His punishments were cruel: the starvation of children, crushing of old men under copes of lead. His court was a brothel where no woman was safe from the royal lust. He laughed at priests even during his coronation. Hell is spoiled by the fouler presence of King John.*

◆ Victorian historians, such as Green, used the medieval chronicles to find out about King John. Roger of Wendover and Matthew Paris were their main sources of information.
◆ Victorians disliked John because of his attitude towards religion and the stories of his many affairs with rich women. They judged John by their own moral standards.
◆ Victorians thought that Magna Carta was very important. They believed that the country should be run in a democratic way, with as many people as possible – not just the king – having a say in how it was governed. Victorians saw Magna Carta as Britain's first step towards becoming a more democratic country.

◆ During this period historians started to study the government records from John's reign in detail. There are far more records from John's reign than from the reigns of previous kings. This meant that historians could find out far more about what the king's government did each day.
◆ Historians started to say that the accounts written by medieval monks were unreliable. They argued that the monks were biased against John, because they were keen supporters of the Pope and the barons. They claimed that the chroniclers had created a myth (an untrue story), which was worthless and very misleading.

**SOURCE 3** Written by David Bates in 1994.

*In some areas John faced impossible difficulties. In others he came close to success. John's failure deserves some sympathy.*

**SOURCE 4** Written by John Gillingham in 1984.

*In fact, John was a very poor king. He was useless at his most important job, managing the barons.*

◆ Modern historians claim that medieval government records give the impression that John was better than he actually was. Just because there are lots of records showing John hard at work does not necessarily mean he worked harder than previous monarchs. Rather, it was not until John's reign that detailed records were kept.
◆ They also point out that he worked harder in England precisely because he was a failure! John had more time to get involved in running England because, by 1204, he had lost his land in France.
◆ They argue that, although monks were prejudiced against John, no one wrote anything that said John was a success.

# ◆ *Contrasting views of King John*

**SOURCE 5** An extract from *A History of England*, written by C.R.L. Fletcher and Rudyard Kipling in 1911.

*The proper heir to the throne was Arthur of Brittany. But John was in England and seized the Crown without much difficulty. John got hold of little Arthur and had him murdered.*

*Then John wasted his time in useless raids in France, while Philip II took control of all John's land in France, except Aquitaine, with perfect ease.*

*The English barons were of course furious with their king. John kept on forcing them to pay enormous sums of money. He would use it to build up a large army, then run away without fighting. When they refused to help him any more, John raved and cursed and practised horrible cruelties on any of his enemies he could catch. John generally behaved in a most unkingly fashion.*

*In 1206, John began a quarrel with the English Church and the Pope. He took away Church property and gave it to a set of foreign favourites. In 1213, he became frightened and gave in to the Pope. This was too much for Englishmen and the country boiled over with rage.*

*The leading barons drew up a list of complaints. Nearly all the towns and most of the churchmen were on their side, yet they were only able to raise a little army of 2,000 men. Luckily John again lost his head and agreed to all their demands. The document he signed was called Magna Carta.*

## ACTIVITY

1 Read Source 5 and answer the following questions:
   **a)** Do the writers believe that John was a bad king? Choose three examples to support your argument.
   **b)** Why do you think Fletcher and Kipling had this opinion of John? Here's a hint: think carefully about when Source 5 was written.
   **c)** Do you think this is a fair account of John's reign? Give examples to support your argument.

**SOURCE 6** An extract from *King John*, written by W.L. Warren in 1961.

*The picture of a monster, put forward by monks such as Roger of Wendover and Matthew Paris, must be rejected forever. John was not the Devil in disguise. Throughout his reign, John's main aim was to rule the land he had inherited in peace.*

*John had the administrative ability of a great ruler but he never got the chance to prove his skills. From the moment he began to rule, rivals and traitors tried to cheat him out of his inheritance. His reaction was one of ruthless determination. Anyone who tried to stop him ruling as his father had done was his enemy, be he baron, King of France or Pope. But as he wrestled with one problem, more enemies sprang up behind his back. Though he sometimes flinched in moments of danger, he never gave up.*

*It was a very difficult task for John to win the support of his barons. He inherited a number of problems. The barons were very unhappy with the way previous kings had ruled the country. Their demands had been ignored for a long time. The barons wanted change. John angered the barons because he tried to keep the power that previous kings had enjoyed.*

**2** Read Source 6 and answer the following questions:
   **a)** Does Warren believe that John was a good monarch? Choose three examples to support your argument.
   **b)** Why do you think Warren's opinion of John is different from the view expressed in Source 5? Don't forget to think carefully about when Source 6 was written.
   **c)** Do you think this is a fair account of John's reign? Give examples to support your argument.

**3** In twenty years' time, do you think that historians' ideas about John will agree with Fletcher and Kipling or with Warren – or neither? Explain why ideas about John might change in the future.

# 1.6 THE HISTORY GRAND PRIX

## Your chance to organise and communicate what you have found out about King John's reputation

### ACTIVITY

It is now time to answer our key question:
**Was John really a bad king?**

Your task is to write an essay that investigates whether John really was a bad king. Begin by deciding which of these arguments is the stronger:

**a)** John was a bad king who made many mistakes and created his own problems.

**b)** John was a good king who was unlucky and inherited many problems.

Writing an essay is like going on a journey. You need to plan carefully and know where you are going (what your conclusion is) before you start. The essay is shown as a Grand Prix on pages 38–39. It has nine stages and you already have notes for many of these. The track and the advice below will help you write your essay. Remember: the argument of your essay must be easy to follow. Your paragraphs should be linked together so that your essay flows smoothly from one point to the next.

Good Luck!

### STAGE 1 — Pre-race Check

Check the clipboard on page 38. Make sure all your answers are 'Yes!' If not, you won't manage the first bend.

### STAGE 2 — The Introduction Bend

The introduction is on the first bend, to remind you that it is surprisingly difficult. Slow down and think carefully about what you are writing.

Key tips:
◆ Make it interesting and lively so that the reader wants to read on.
◆ Keep it short, but make sure the reader knows what your answer will be.

Example:
King John is one of the most well-known figures in history because. . .
Many people think that John was. . .
However, some people disagree with this view of John.
They argue that. . .
My view is. . .

### STAGE 3 — The Bad King Straight (page 8)

Here you are using evidence to support an argument. This is usually quite straightforward. You might be able to speed up.

Key tip:
◆ Each argument should be supported by at least one piece of evidence.

Example:
Medieval monks argued that John was a cruel king. For example, Roger of Wendover. . .
They also claimed that. . .
For example. . .

### STAGE 4 — The Evidence Chicane (pages 12–13)

This is where things start to get difficult. You need to point out the weaknesses in the evidence that says John was a bad king. Take this stage carefully. Don't rush, or you'll spin off.

Key tip:
◆ If you argue that evidence is unreliable you must explain why it is unreliable and give examples to support this view.

Examples:
When we examine the evidence that shows John as a bad king we have to be careful because. . .
For example. . .
This is unreliable because. . .

 **The Inheritance Straight** (pages 14–19)
Here, you are using evidence to support an argument, as in Stage 3.

Key tips:
- Don't just list John's problems. Explain why each problem caused him difficulties.
- It helps if you place the problems in order of importance.

Examples:
John inherited many problems when he became king. The main problem was. . .
This was a major problem because. . .
A second problem was. . .
This meant that. . .

 **John's Reign Chicane** (pages 20–28)
You need to weigh the evidence and make a decision: was he a good, a bad or an unlucky ruler? Make sure that you approach this evidence chicane with great care. You could crash!

Key tip:
- Do not look at just one side of the story. Look at the strengths and weaknesses of all three arguments.

Example:
There is a lot of evidence to suggest that John was a bad king. For example. . .
However, John can also be seen as an unlucky ruler. For example. . .
There is also evidence that John was a good ruler. For example. . .

**STAGE 7** **The High Speed Historiography Hairpin** (pages 30–35)
After you have completed Stage 6 you can either go straight to your conclusion or take on the High Speed Historiography Hairpin.

Key tip:
- Don't just describe how interpretations of John have changed since the Middle Ages. You also need to explain why they have changed.

Examples:
Interpretations of John have changed a great deal since the Middle Ages. In Tudor times. . .
This was because. . .
In contrast, the Victorians thought that. . .

**STAGE 8** **Conclusion Corner**

Key tips:
- Keep your conclusion brief. Avoid repeating at length what you have already written.
- Answer the question and explain the key reasons why you have reached this conclusion.
- Include words or phrases from the question in your conclusion.

Examples:
Having examined all the evidence, I conclude that John was/was not a bad king.
This is because. . .

**STAGE 9** **The Finishing Straight**
Do not miss out Stage 9. By this point in the race you will have put a great deal of effort into your essay. Do not spoil everything by handing in a piece of work which has lots of mistakes in it. Check your essay carefully. Improve parts that you are not happy with.

**Ten top tips for revising and editing**
Creative suggestions:
1. Do you think the writing is interesting/enjoyable to read?
2. Is there anything missing? Have you supported all your arguments with evidence?
3. Is there anything that isn't clear or accurate?
4. Have you answered the actual question?
5. Is your work neatly presented? Do you want to add a front cover or illustrate your work?

Technical suggestions:
6. Use a dictionary to check the spelling of any words that you are not sure of.
7. Full stops must be used at the end of every sentence. Have you used full stops regularly?
8. Check that you have used capital letters to start names, as well as every new sentence.
9. Check that you have written in paragraphs. Have you left an indent (started your writing 2.5 cm from the margin) at the beginning of each new paragraph?
10. Check the length of your sentences. Put in some short, sharp sentences. It adds variety and interest.

Stage 3: **THE BAD KING STRAIGHT**
a) Explain why many people think that John was a bad king.
b) Give examples of the bad things John is supposed to have done.

Stage 4: **THE EVIDENCE CHICANE**
Highlight the problems with the evidence that suggests John was a bad king:
a) Explain why the evidence might be unreliable.
b) Provide examples of unreliable evidence.

Stage 5: **THE INHERITANCE STRAIGHT**
a) Explain the problems that John inherited.
b) Explain how difficult these problems were.

Stage 9: **THE FINISHING STRAIGHT**
Revising and editing:
Check your work carefully. Use the ten top tips on page 37 to improve areas that you are not happy with.

1500 and beyond

# WHAT HAPPENED AFTER JOHN?

A citizenship and history overview of kings and Parliament in the Middle Ages

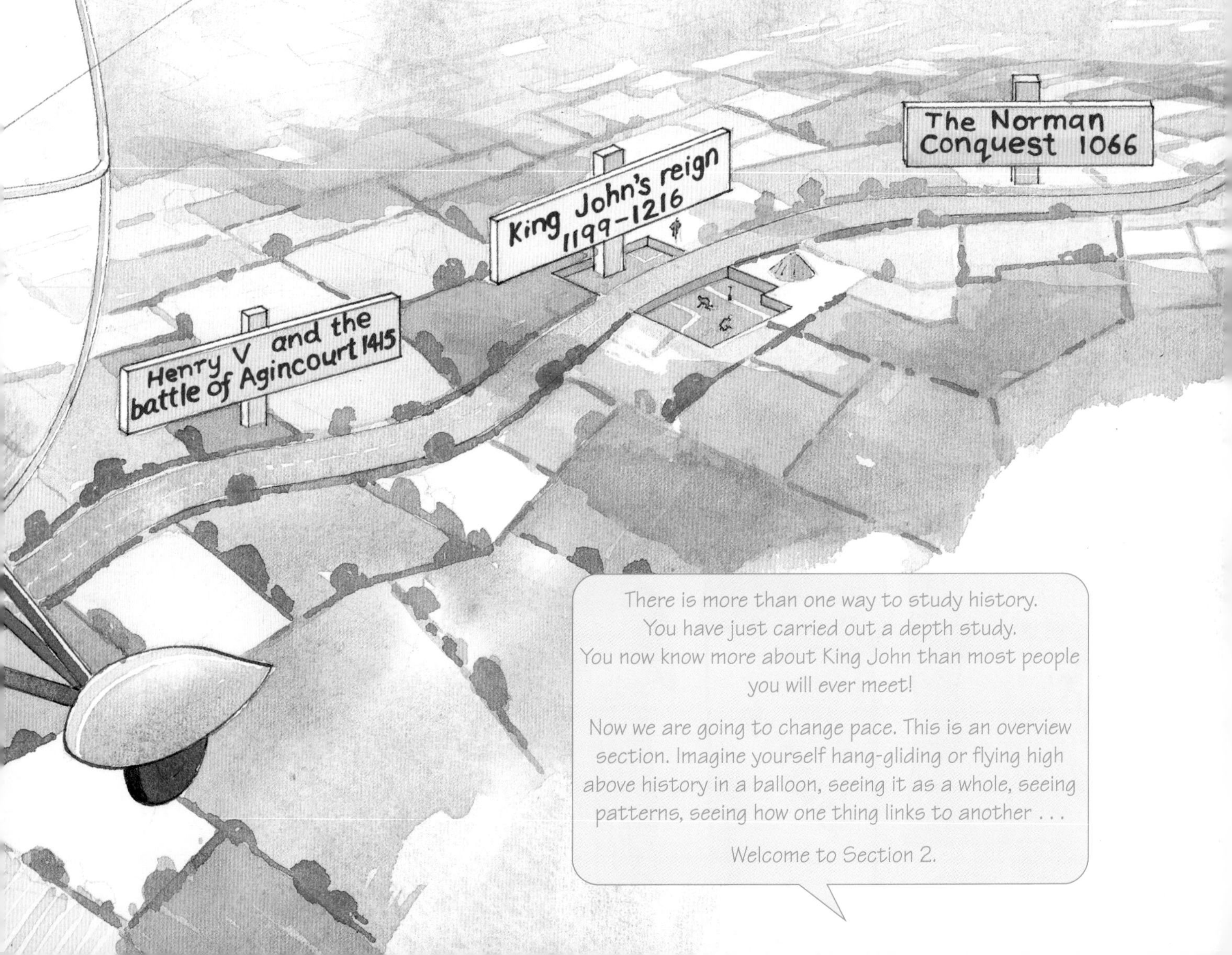

Henry V and the battle of Agincourt 1415

King John's reign 1199–1216

The Norman Conquest 1066

There is more than one way to study history. You have just carried out a depth study. You now know more about King John than most people you will ever meet!

Now we are going to change pace. This is an overview section. Imagine yourself hang-gliding or flying high above history in a balloon, seeing it as a whole, seeing patterns, seeing how one thing links to another . . .

Welcome to Section 2.

# 2.1 HE THINKS IT'S ALL OVER – BUT IS IT?
Find out whether Magna Carta really stopped
kings ruling the country

## ◆ Who was in charge in John's day?

*"Welcome to the second part of my
book. I'm as puzzled about this part as
you are because it's all about what
happened after I died! Some people
say that after Magna Carta kings lost
power and it's my fault . I want you to
find out for me whether that's right.
Before you begin, make sure you are
clear about how the country was ruled in my
day and how that is different from today."*

### ACTIVITY

1 Look at the cartoon. Which statement best
describes how England was ruled around 1200?
a) Parliament ruled the country.
b) The barons ruled the country.
c) The king ruled the country in whatever way
he wanted.
d) The king ruled the country with the barons'
help and advice.
2 Explain why you think one statement is correct
and why the other three statements are incorrect.
3 As a class, try to find the connection between
the pictures on the opposite page.

I make all the important decisions about law, tax and war. Sometimes I call the barons and bishops to a council to ask their advice. However, I can run the country without asking anyone for advice.

We give the king advice . . . when he asks for it. We are very rich and powerful so it is risky for the king to ignore us. We can always rebel, as some kings have found out to their cost!

Our barons give us land and in return we fight for them. Some of us own lots of land, but we don't have a say in how the king rules the country. We are rarely invited to a council.

Who ruled the country in King John's time? You can see from this cartoon who had a say in government – and who did not!

I am a merchant. We make a great deal of money from trade. We pay taxes but are never invited to a council. We have very little power.

I work on a farm and people like me make up 95 per cent of the population. We grow all the food, but we have no say in how the country is governed.

Monarch

Barons

Knights

People

## Find the connection!

These four pictures have something in common. What is it?

1640s: King fights Parliament. Who will rule the country?

1840s: Millions sign Charter. Every man wants the chance to vote for a Member of Parliament.

1913: Death at the races. SUFFRAGETTE dies for the right to vote for her Member of Parliament.

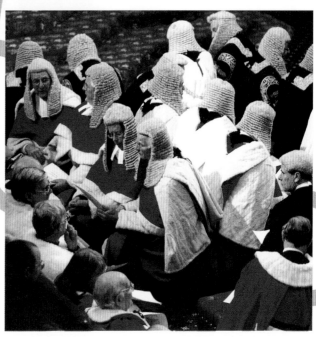

2000: The Commons discuss abolishing the Lords. Another battle over Parliament.

# ◆ Who is in charge today?

The connection between the four pictures on the previous page is **Parliament**. John will be very confused by this answer because there was no such thing as Parliament when he was alive. In John's day kings were expected to ask for advice from their barons and bishops, but it was the king who actually ruled the country. And no king ever thought of asking the ordinary people how he should rule.

Today, things are very different.

## ACTIVITY

1 Look back at the cartoon on page 42. Now look at the cartoon below, which shows how Britain is governed today. Ask your teacher for a copy and fill in the empty speech bubbles.

> I have to agree to the plans put forward by the Prime Minister and the House of Commons. I don't have any real power. I basically do as I am told.

PRIME MINISTER

Members of the House of Commons

Members of the House of Lords

Monarch

PEOPLE

2 Compare the two cartoons.
   a) What are the differences between government now and government in 1200?
   b) What are the similarities between government now and government in 1200?

3 Medieval monarchs had a great deal of power. This was shown on their seals (see Source 1). Draw or describe your design for the seal of a modern monarch. You should use symbols to illustrate the role that the monarch has in Britain today.

**SOURCE 1** King John's seal. The front shows King John holding an orb and sceptre in his left hand and a sword in his right. This illustrates the king's responsibilities as ruler (orb), judge (sceptre), and protector of the Church (sword). The reverse shows King John on horseback. He is holding a shield in his left hand and a sword in his right. This illustrates the king's responsibilities as a warrior.

## ◆ *How did we get from there to here?*

In 1200, kings were in charge and there was no such thing as a Prime Minister or Parliament. Now the Prime Minister and Parliament rule the country and the monarch has no real power at all. Some people even think it would be a good idea to abolish the monarchy altogether.

But **when** did Parliament become more important than the monarch? It will take some time to answer this question, and you might not find out the answer in this book. However, over the next few pages, you will find out whether that vital change happened in the Middle Ages. The story of the transfer of power from the monarch to Parliament begins during the reign of King John, but . . .

**Did Magna Carta stop kings ruling the country...**

or were kings still in control in 1500 (which is as far as this book goes)?

Like John, you might be thinking: 'What's this got to do with me?' Good question! Stick with it and you'll see.

On the way we'll do our best to make this investigation as interesting as possible, with lots of quick activities that will make you think hard. And, you'll have irascible old John to help you on your way. Irascible – now

that's a good word. It's difficult to spell but if you use it you'll impress a lot of people. Ask your teacher if you want to know what it means: but whatever you do, don't accuse him or her of being irascible or you'll find out the meaning the hard way!

Now, John's waiting for you on the next page and he's got his own ideas about what happened after Magna Carta. Don't keep him waiting. You know what he's like – irascible!

CIVIL WAR 1640's

QUEEN VICTORIA 1837-1901

2000

**Or here?**

**Or here?**

47

# ◆ *King John's first question: who started Parliament?*

*"What happened to kings and Parliament after Magna Carta? I've already got a couple of theories. This is what I think . . .*

*The barons started Parliament. It makes sense! No king would have come up with the idea. I think that the barons became more confident after they forced me to agree to Magna Carta. They started Parliament which then took away the king's power.*

*I must have been the last king with any real power."*

## ACTIVITY

It is now time to find out if the first part of John's theory is correct and the barons really did start Parliament. Once you have read the reports on the suspects, write your own report to King John. Don't forget to explain whether or not you agree with his theory before you tell him your own theory.

## Suspect number 1

**Name:** *Simon de Montfort, baron*

### When?

In the 1250s, during Henry III's reign (1216–1272).

### Why?

Henry III was King John's son. He was extravagant and untrustworthy. He upset the barons by demanding high taxes. He also gave all the important jobs to his wife's French relatives. The barons felt they were being ignored.

### What happened?

By 1258, the barons, led by Simon de Montfort, were determined to make Henry change his ways and keep to Magna Carta. They forced him to agree that a council of fifteen barons should govern the country and that there should be regular meetings of barons called parliaments. However, Henry broke the agreement and this started a civil war.

In 1264, Henry was captured at the battle of Lewes and Simon took over the running of the country. He called a parliament. He invited the barons and bishops who were on his side. He also invited two knights from each county and two merchants from each of the large towns, because he realised that he needed the support of as many rich men as possible in his war against Henry.

### Did it last?

No, this new type of parliament did not last long. In 1265, Simon de Montfort was killed by Henry's son, Edward, at the battle of Evesham. With Edward's help, Henry soon regained control of the country. Parliament did not meet regularly, and, when it did meet, it was just like the councils which had taken place in King John's reign because only bishops and barons were invited.

### KEY QUESTIONS

1 Why did the barons oppose Henry III?
2 How was the parliament called by Simon de Montfort different from earlier meetings?
3 Did this type of parliament go on to meet regularly?

# Suspect number 2

**Name:** *King Edward I*

## What happened?

Edward knew that the barons and wealthy merchants were more likely to agree to taxes if they could discuss them with the king. It was also easier for Edward if he could talk to everyone at once about taxes. In 1295, he invited representatives from the towns and the counties, as well as the barons and bishops, to a parliament. His parliament was called the Model Parliament. It was made up of Lords (barons and bishops) and Commons (knights and merchants).

## Did it last?

Yes! Edward I called Parliament many times after 1295 because it was very useful to him. It was a convenient way to get people to agree to taxation. Edward was still firmly in control of government. Parliament met when he wanted it to and it discussed what he wanted it to. Parliament continued to meet regularly after Edward's death, because later kings needed money as badly as he had.

## When?

Edward I ruled from 1272 to 1307. He was Henry III's son.

## Why?

Edward was energetic, cunning and tough. The barons obeyed and respected him. He made them feel that they were involved in running the country. He also improved law and order.

Edward was a very good military leader. He conquered Wales and regained the whole of Gascony in France. By the time he died he had almost completely conquered Scotland. However, all these wars meant that he always needed to collect taxes. Unlike today, people did not pay tax every year. They only paid taxes for special events, usually wars. This meant that if there were no wars they might not pay tax for several years.

## KEY QUESTIONS

1 Why was Parliament set up during Edward I's reign?
2 Did Edward I's Parliament continue to meet regularly?
3 Who was in control of Edward I's Parliament – the barons or the King?
4 Is King John's theory right? Did the barons start regular meetings of Parliament? Explain why you agree or disagree?

## ◆ *King John's second question: did kings lose all their power?*

*"So, I was wrong about Parliament! It was my grandson, Edward I, who started regular meetings of Parliament. He sounds like a tough, clever king to control Parliament. But what happened after Edward? Here's my second question: did kings lose all their power after that? My theory is that once Parliament got going kings didn't have any power left."*

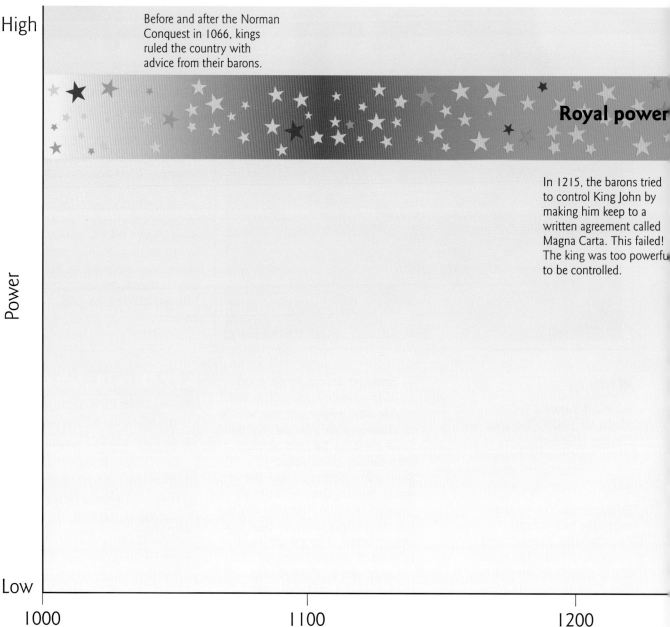

High

Before and after the Norman Conquest in 1066, kings ruled the country with advice from their barons.

**Royal power**

In 1215, the barons tried to control King John by making him keep to a written agreement called Magna Carta. This failed! The king was too powerful to be controlled.

Power

Low

1000             1100             1200

## ACTIVITY

1 Look carefully at the timeline, and think about royal power and the power of Parliament.
   **a)** What stayed the same between 1000 and 1500?
   **b)** What changed?
2 The barons tried three methods of controlling the power of the king.
   **a)** What were the three methods?
   **b)** Did any of them succeed?
3 Do you agree with King John's theory that he was the last king with any real power? Think about whether kings had lost all their power to Parliament by 1500. Then write a report to King John explaining why you agree or disagree with him.

In the 1260s, the barons again tried to control a king. This time it was Henry III. They held meetings, called parliaments, so that they could run the country. This failed too. The king was still too powerful to be controlled.

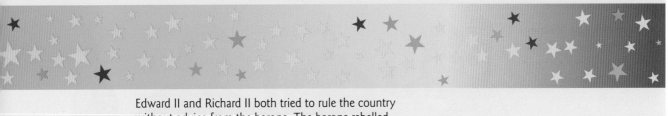

Edward II and Richard II both tried to rule the country without advice from the barons. The barons rebelled against them both. The barons won, but they were still faced with the problem of how to control the king. If, at any point, the king regained control he would execute the rebels. They realised that the only way to control a king was to execute him and choose a new king. This is why both Edward and Richard were deposed.

Parliament met regularly during the 1300s and 1400s. England was at war with France and kings needed Parliament to agree to taxes. In return, kings listened to complaints from Parliament and were willing to agree to requests. The knights and merchants (the Commons) attended more and more regularly. By 1337, Edward III had agreed that whenever the Lords met, the Commons should also meet. They met in separate rooms and this is how we get the names the 'House of Commons' and the 'House of Lords'.

Parliament in 1500 was very different from Parliament today:
• The king was firmly in control. He only called Parliament when he needed it and it only met for a few weeks at a time.
• The House of Commons had little real power. It was expected to agree to the king's plans for taxation, but it rarely discussed important issues such as foreign policy.
• The House of Lords was far more powerful than the House of Commons. The barons and the bishops were the wealthiest people in the country and could influence the king's decisions.
• Only the rich could vote for Members of Parliament. 95 per cent of the population had no say in how the country was governed.

## Power of Parliament

Edward I held the first regular meetings of Parliament so that he could get agreement for taxes to fund his wars more easily.

1300          1400          1500

Time

# ◆ Why did the power of the monarchy stay so high?

"I'm glad to see that the king was still the most powerful person in the country in 1500. All those people who said I was a bad king because I agreed to Magna Carta and gave away the king's power to the barons were wrong ... very wrong!"

## ACTIVITY

The picture below shows you the reasons why the power of the king stayed so high throughout the Middle Ages. When you have had a good look at it, turn to the opposite page and look at the medallists. Do you agree that these were probably the most important reasons why kings stayed powerful during the Middle Ages?

Kings are God's deputies on earth. Kings are chosen by God to rule over us. At his coronation the new king is anointed with holy oil to show that his power came straight from God. Anyone rebelling against the king is also rebelling against God.

The king is by far the richest man in the country. He can collect taxes whenever he needs money for war. Nobody else has a fortune to rival the king's.

The king has officials all over the country. They send him news as quickly as possible so that he knows what is going on and can stay in control.

RELIGION

WEALTH

WAR

COMMUNICATION

The country is often at war. We need to defend our land and we need one man to lead and organise our armies. To fight wars we need an heroic leader, not a committee, to decide what to do.

GOVERNMENT

NO ALTERNATIVE

No one can think of any other way of running the country. If a king is deposed he is still replaced by another king! Every country has a king. If only I could think of another system, but I can't.

The king has many officials helping him run the country. We send orders and keep records, which helps the king stay in control.

# HE THINKS IT'S ALL OVER – AGAIN!

## Find out whether anyone ever won back John's lost empire

*"I might have been wrong about the last investigation but I won't be wrong again. I cannot believe that any other king could have re-conquered the land I lost in France. If I couldn't do it, who could?"*

## ACTIVITY

Play the game to find out if John's lost empire was ever recovered.

**a)** Get into groups of three. You each need a counter or marker to move around the board.

**b)** Choose one king each, and place your counter on his starting square.

**c)** Take it in turns to move one square each, following the instructions in the squares as you go. Add up all the points your king scores.

**d)** Keep a note of your final scores and repeat the game with the remaining kings.

**e)** Look at the total score for each king. The king with the highest number of points wins. He was the most successful soldier. Why did this king score so many points?

John (1199–1216)
Start at square 17

Edward I (1272–1307)
Start at square 23

Edward II (1307–1327)
Start at square 21

Edward III (1327–1377)
Start at square 13

Henry V (1413–1422)
Start at square 11

Henry VI (1422–1461)
Start at square 14

# Which king was the most successful soldier?

**1** Wales conquered! Edward I won control of all of Wales, and built castles to ensure English control. Gain 8 points. Now add up Edward I's points.

**2** Agincourt – the greatest victory of the Middle Ages! Henry V's tiny army beat the French, and Henry conquered northern France. Gain 10 points. Go to square 24.

**3** Our hero! Edward III won great victories against the French, and even captured the King of France. However, the French fought back hard when Edward grew old. Gain 7 points. Now add up Edward III's points.

**4** Edward I kept control of Gascony, in the south of France, despite strong opposition. Gain 4 points. Go to square 1.

**5** Getting worse! Scottish armies invaded the north of England because Henry VI was such a poor soldier. Lose 4 points. Go to square 12 – if you dare!

**6** Pathetic! Edward II gave away some English lands in the south of France. Lose 2 points. Now add up Edward II's points.

**7** More success! The English already controlled south Wales. John defeated the princes of north Wales. He did not, however, win lasting control of Wales. Gain 4 points. Go to square 9.

**8** Bannockburn. Edward II's army was crushed by the Scots at the battle of Bannockburn in 1314. This ended English chances of conquering Scotland. Lose 8 points. Go to square 20.

**9** Disaster! John lost Normandy and the rest of his land in France. Lose 10 points. Now add up John's points.

**10** Edward III kept firm control of Wales. Gain 4 points. Go to square 3 and prepare for victory.

**11** Early success! Henry V led armies to put down the Welsh rebellion when he was still a young prince. Gain 8 points. Go to square 2 and get ready to cheer.

**12** The worst square of all! Henry VI lost all the French land his father, Henry V, had won. This was a worse disaster than John's defeat in France. Lose 10 points. Now add up Henry VI's points.

**13** A strong start. Edward III captured the King of Scots in battle but did not try to conquer Scotland. He was too busy fighting in France. Gain 5 points. Go to square 22.

**14** Henry VI kept control of Wales, thanks to loyal nobles, but that's the highlight of his reign. Gain 3 points. Go to square 19.

**15** Another success! The King of Scots gave John hostages and agreed that John was his overlord. Gain 2 points. Go to square 7.

**16** They didn't dare! Ireland did not cause Henry V any trouble. Gain 2 points. Now add up Henry V's points.

**17** Surprise! John led an expedition to Ireland and increased English control. He also built a royal castle near Dublin. Gain 4 points. Go to square 15.

**18** Edward I won several battles against the Scots and claimed to be overlord, but he never won complete control of Scotland. Gain 6 points. Go to square 4.

**19** Henry VI allowed his enemies to build up support in Ireland. Lose 2 points. Go to square 5.

**20** More trouble! The Irish allied with the Scots against Edward II. They nearly drove the English out of Ireland. Lose 3 points. Go to square 6.

**21** Edward II was the very first Prince of Wales, and he kept control of Wales thanks to his father's castles. Gain 2 points. Go to square 8.

**22** Ireland did not cause Edward III trouble, so he was able to concentrate on his war in France. Gain 2 points. Go to square 10.

**23** Edward I kept control of English land in Ireland, but did not completely control the country. Gain 2 points. Go to square 18.

**24** Prisoner! The Scots tried to help the French against Henry V, but they did not succeed. Henry kept the King of Scots prisoner. Gain 4 points. Go to square 16.

# ◆ Why did John's successors struggle to regain his lost empire?

**Geography**
The mountains of north Wales and Scotland were difficult for English armies to cross. Local soldiers knew this difficult terrain better than English soldiers.

"You'll have to agree that I might not have been the best soldier ever to be King of England, but I certainly wasn't the worst. And, it was my grandson, Edward I, who nearly won control of the whole of Britain around 1300. He did so well that the English chronicler, Peter Langtoft, wrote the poem you can see on the map. I'm very proud of my grandson, although it's a pity Langtoft was exaggerating. Even Edward I could not completely control Scotland.

I wish I'd had Henry V to help me against France. I wonder what the secret of his success at Agincourt was?"

**Wealth**
The Kings of England were much richer than the other kings in Britain, but even so the cost of trying to conquer the rest of Britain was very high.

**Distance**
The cost of sending armies the long distances to Scotland and Ireland was very high. Wales was closer and therefore easier and cheaper to control.

The English control the Pale around Dublin, but they do not control all of Ireland. They seem to have given up trying to conquer the rest.

King John's castle near Dublin.

Dublin

Irish Pale

## ACTIVITY

1 Look at the boxes on the map.
   **a)** Which reasons helped the English conquer Wales?
   **b)** Which reasons prevented the English completely controlling Scotland and Ireland?
2 Did any English king ever re-conquer France?
3 What do you think was the main reason why later kings struggled to regain the empire John had lost?

It seemed like the end of the world when Edward I built his castles all over Wales, but we've tried to fight back. We rebelled under Owain Glyndwr. The English always seem to be too strong though.

The Declaration of Arbroath, written in 1320, says that 'As long as a hundred men are left we will never submit to the power of the English. We do not fight for glory, riches or honour but only for liberty.' I'm proud to say that Scotland has been an independent kingdom ever since King Robert the Bruce beat the English at Bannockburn in 1314.

The monument to <u>William Wallace in Stirling.</u>

Stirling

✕

Bannockburn

**Leadership**
There were many different princes in Wales and Ireland, and they often fought each other. This helped the English. In contrast, the Scots were united behind one king, especially after Edward I tried to conquer Scotland.

Now are the islanders all joined together
And Scotland reunited to the kingdom.
Wales is in King Edward's power
And Ireland is under his control.
There is no king or prince in these countries
Except King Edward who has united them all.

Glyndwr's
Parliament House
in <u>Machynllech.</u>

Machynllech

**France**
Powerful kings, like Edward III and Henry V, were more interested in fighting in France than in Britain. French kings helped the Scots to distract the English from invading France.

The English had great victories during the HUNDRED YEARS WAR but we won in the end. The battle of Agincourt in 1415 was a disaster for the French, but we fought back and threw the English out of France again in 1453.

<u>Kidwelly Castle, South Wales.</u>

**Technology**
English kings had better equipment and weapons than their British enemies because they were richer.
They also used the latest ideas about defence to build huge castles like Kidwelly Castle in Wales.
These castles were nearly impossible to capture.

Agincourt

## ◆ *A great English victory: the battle of Agincourt*

In August 1415, Henry V sailed for France with an army of over 9000 men. As his fleet left the coast behind, swans were seen swimming among the ships. This was a sign of good fortune; but it took a long time for good fortune to arrive.

As soon as he landed in France, Henry attacked the town of Harfleur. He hoped to capture it in a few days and then march gloriously across northern France, before beating the French in a great battle. These plans went hopelessly wrong. It took a month to capture Harfleur and in that time over 2000 English soldiers died, mostly from disease. Many of the rest were seriously ill. What was Henry to do now? Abandon his plans of glory and go home to build up his army for another invasion? Or . . . we'll let one of the priests who travelled with Henry's army take up the story. After all, he saw it happen with his own eyes. He wrote his account down in a book called *The Deeds of King Henry V.*

The King decided to march through Normandy to Calais, a hundred miles distant, even though dysentery had killed far more of our men than had the sword. We had but 900 knights and 5000 archers fit to fight. Commanding the army to take stores for eight days, he fearlessly began the march on Tuesday 8 October.

On the Sunday we came to the town of Abbeville, where we hoped to cross the River Somme. There our scouts told us that the bridges had been broken. Dejected, we moved on, only to find more bridges broken and a great French army in battle formation on the far side of the river. Faint with hunger we expected to be overwhelmed by this huge enemy. I, who am writing this, and many others looked in bitterness to Heaven, calling on St George to ask God to help us. Without any other hope, we hurried on, searching for a way across the river so that we could reach Calais.

Suddenly, by God's will, the King was told of a ford across the river. Immediately, King Henry sent a force of knights and archers across the river to protect the rest of the army while it crossed. We started our crossing at about one o'clock and it was only an hour short of nightfall before we were all across. We spent a cheerful night, hoping that the French army would not follow us any further.

Next day, we found the roads quite remarkably churned up by a French army, many thousands strong. Fearing battle, we raised our hearts and eyes to Heaven, crying out for God to have pity on us and save us from death.

We moved onwards. On 24 October we saw, about half a mile away, the grim-looking ranks of the French army. They filled the fields like a countless swarm of locusts. Our King, very calmly and quite heedless of danger, encouraged his army and drew them up for immediate action. Then every man confessed his sins to God. One knight, Sir Walter Hungerford, said to the King that he wished he had an extra 10,000 of the best archers in England. 'That is a foolish way to talk', said the King, 'I would not have a single man more than I do. These I have with me are God's people. Don't you believe that God will be able to overcome the French?'

The enemy watched us. As darkness fell, we could hear the French calling out to their friends and servants. It is said they were so sure of victory that they threw dice for our King and his nobles.

On the morrow, Friday 25 October, the Feast of Saints Crispin and Crispinian, the French stood in their battle lines across our road to Calais, in the field of Agincourt. The number of them was truly terrifying. They placed squadrons of cavalry, hundreds strong, on each flank, to break down our archers. Their vanguard consisted of dismounted knights, the pick of their forces, with a forest of spears and gleaming helmets, with more cavalry on their flanks. They had thirty times more than all our men put together.

Our King, after praising God, made ready for the battle. He drew up a single battle line of knights and placed wedges of archers among the knights. The archers drove sharpened stakes into the ground in front of them to stop the French cavalry charge. I and the other priests prayed to God. I was sitting on a horse among the baggage at the rear of the battle. The French cavalry charged against our archers but they were forced back under the stinging hail of arrows. Many were also stopped by the stakes in the ground. Then the French nobility advanced on foot, but, afraid of our arrows which pierced their visors and helmets, they broke into three columns and attacked our line in three places. They hurled themselves against our men and threw them back almost a spear's length.

Then the battle raged at its fiercest. Our archers notched their arrows and loosed them into the enemy's flanks and, when all their arrows had been fired, they seized axes, swords and spears and struck and stabbed at the enemy. God increased our men's strength, which had been weakened by lack of food and illness. Fear and trembling seized the French. There was such a great pile of the dead that our men climbed up onto the heaps and butchered their enemies down below. After two or three hours, the French were put to flight.

In that great French army died three dukes, five counts, more than 90 barons, over 1500 knights and 4–5000 others. Out of our little band there were found dead on the field no more than nine or ten persons, as well as the duke of York and the earl of Suffolk and two new knights. No prince ever commanded his people on the march with more bravery and consideration or performed greater feats of strength in battle. No king ever achieved so much in so short a time or returned home with so great and glorious a triumph. To God alone be the honour and glory, for ever and ever. Amen.

An English longbowman from the time of Agincourt. The best archers could fire ten to twelve arrows each minute for a distance of 275 metres. Henry's 5000 archers could fire at least 50,000 arrows into the packed ranks of the 20,000 strong French army every minute.

Many people think that armour was so heavy that knights had to be winched into their saddles and could not move if they fell to the ground. Nonsense! Armour was dangerous because the wearer became very hot and dehydrated in battle and therefore became weaker and lost concentration. But a fully-armoured knight could mount his own horse, roll over and stand up if he fell, and the fittest could even do handstands.

# ◆ *Postscript: why is Henry V a hero?*

What was it like to read about a hero at last, after all the time studying that old villain, King John?

English heroes don't come much more heroic than Henry V! He's been worshipped as a great hero ever since the battle of Agincourt. Books, plays, films – you name them he's starred in them. So, now that you are an expert in historical reputation, spend a moment thinking about heroes.

## ACTIVITY A

You know that John's reputation as a villain has been affected by many different factors. It is the same with heroes. Why is Henry V viewed as such a hero? Is it simply because he won a battle one October day in 1415, or is it more complicated than that?

Look at the reasons given below. Place them in order of importance.

**Because we like stories about the English winning wars.** In the 1300s and 1400s England was at war with France and Scotland. The victory at Agincourt helped to bring people together as a nation.

**Because Henry V was an inspirational leader.** He fought alongside his men and encouraged them. The battle of Agincourt teaches us never to give up, even when things look very bad.

**Because Henry V died young.** After Agincourt Henry conquered northern France. He was very successful, but he died before he could make too many mistakes. His hopeless son was left to make them for him. Henry VI lost all the land Henry V had won.

## Why is Henry V a hero?

**Because Henry V was the first really English hero.** Henry and his father were the first English kings to speak English as their first language. This gave the English people a sense of national identity.

*Je suis Jean, roi d'Angleterre.*

*I am Henry, King of England.*

**Because of Shakespeare.** England's most famous writer wrote three plays about Henry. In *Henry IV (Parts One and Two)* he shows the young Henry as a wild teenager. But in *Henry V*, Henry has grown into a heroic, daring, brilliant leader. These plays kept Henry's reputation as a hero alive.

*Here's a good story. People will love this one.*

## ACTIVITY B

1 Choose one person from history that you regard as a hero or heroine.
2 Make a list of reasons why you think that person is a hero.
3 Compile a class list of what makes someone a hero and decide which you think is the most important reason.

## Why have interpretations of Henry V and the battle of Agincourt changed?

Henry was certainly a hero and the battle of Agincourt was seen as a wonderful victory by English people at the time and by Shakespeare. But later events can change the way we think about a battle or a person. You have seen how interpretations of King John changed over time. Now look at Sources 1 and 2.

> This story shall the good man teach his son: From this day to the ending of the world, ... we [who fought] in it shall be remembered;

**SOURCE 1**

**SOURCE 2**

# ACTIVITY C

As a class, discuss the following questions.

1 In what ways do Sources 1 and 2 give you different ideas about the battle of Agincourt?

2 Read Captions A and B.

**Caption A**
This film of *Henry V* was made by one of Britain's most famous actors in 1989. By this time people had grown used to seeing pictures of real war taking place in Vietnam and the Falkland Islands on their televisions. So this film focuses on the pain, suffering and death at the battle of Agincourt.

**Caption B**
This film of *Henry V* was made by one of Britain's most famous actors in 1944, during the Second World War. In 1944 British and allied troops invaded France, the first stage in beating Hitler's German army. The film avoids showing the reality of warfare. Even during battle scenes few soldiers are shown dying or wounded, even among the French.

Which do you think belongs to which film? Explain your choice.

3 Why have interpretations of the battle of Agincourt changed?

4 Now that you have read the story of the battle of Agincourt, do you think that the story should be taught and remembered in schools today? Why?

5 Choose one other event or person that you have studied in this book and explain why he, she or it should be remembered in the future.

6 Even in 1415 there were different ideas about the battle of Agincourt and about Henry V. People's attitudes changed depending on who they were. There were many ways of telling the story of the battle of Agincourt. Re-tell the story from the viewpoint of one of the following:
   a) A French soldier who was on the losing side.
   b) An English archer telling the story to his friends as soon as he arrives home.
   c) Two English soldiers discussing the battle 40 years after Henry had died and his son had lost all his land in France.
   d) An English widow whose husband died during the battle.

"I hope you've learnt a lot from this Section. I certainly have. Clearly, the king was the master in the Middle Ages. Parliament had been created but it didn't take away any royal power. Kings were still firmly in control in 1500. The barons tried to destroy royal power ... but they failed.

I must say I'm disappointed that no one conquered the rest of Britain after my death. It should have been an easy task. After all, I'd done all the hard work. The kings that followed me must have been poor soldiers or very lazy. No one repeated my successes in Wales, Scotland and Ireland.

Later monarchs also struggled to reconquer France. A few kings won the odd battle here and there, but no one came close to regaining the land that Philip II of France stole from me. I may have failed in France (because of all that bad luck), but so did every other English king. Not that I am very surprised. If I couldn't control France, who could?"

## ACTIVITY

1 On your own copy of John's summary:
   a) mark all the statements that you think are accurate or fair in blue
   b) mark all the statements that you think are inaccurate or unfair in red.
2 Briefly explain why each of the statements in red is inaccurate or unfair.
3 Which of the following statements do you agree with?
   a) John is mainly telling lies about what happened after his death.
   b) Most of what John says is fair and accurate, but he does exaggerate a few points.
   c) John is being very selective. He has only chosen information that makes himself look good.
4 Write your own summary of what happened after John's death. Your summary must be no longer than 200 words.

We began by asking you to investigate whether John really was a bad king. To answer that question you had to learn a lot about the Middle Ages. Then you investigated the changes that took place after John's death, which meant finding out lots more about the medieval period. You must now feel like a real expert in medieval history.

The next activity gives you the chance to test your knowledge. Don't panic! You don't have to answer any more questions. This is just a chance for you to realise how much you have learnt. There are also some questions that you won't be able to answer yet . . . but that you'll know all about once you have studied later periods of history.

**ACTIVITY**

Look at the picture below:
a) Which questions can you answer after working through this book?
b) Which questions remain unanswered?

## ACTIVITY A

The Activities in this book have been designed to improve your
historical skills.
1 Look carefully at the History Skills Wall.
   **a)** Which new skills have you learned through studying this book?
   **b)** Which skills have you improved?
   **c)** Which skills do you need to develop further?
2 Before you begin your next history topic, design an action plan for
  yourself. Set yourself three targets to improve your work in history
  and list the skills that you will need to practise to reach these targets.

# The History Skills Wall

I organise my research effectively using sorting frames.

I know which questions to ask to check the reliability of sources.

I understand why historical interpretations change over time.

I can plan an essay effectively.

I revise and edit my work thoroughly.

I know how to make speeches to an audience.

I know what makes a good paragraph.

I can decide which information is relevant to an enquiry.

I think for myself and form my own opinions.

I support my argument with evidence.

I know how to weigh conflicting evidence in order to reach a conclusion.

I can write effective introductions and conclusions.

I can identify changes and continuities over time.

I can explain why an event happened by discussing several reasons, not just one.

I check the evidence before believing what I see or read.

## ACTIVITY B

1 The skills you have developed throughout this book will help you become better at history. However, you will also be able to use them in other subjects. Which skills from The History Skills Wall are useful in other subjects?

2 These skills are of use in a wide range of careers too. History gives you the skills that many employers want. Here are two examples. How many more can you think of?

History is about investigating. Historians collect evidence from a range of different sources and use it to form their own opinions.

Many jobs require you to compare arguments, to sort through lots of information and reach a conclusion about what to do.

History teaches you how to communicate your ideas to other people in a clear and well-organised way. It also shows you how to use evidence to support your arguments, which gives you a better chance of convincing people that you are right.

Lots of jobs want you to explain things to people, to present and justify your decisions in a report or a speech.

"It's time to say goodbye. I hope you enjoyed the investigations in this book. History's interesting. It's the only subject that looks at individuals, that lets you find out about real people and how they lived their lives. In future history lessons you will find out about more exciting characters. Some of them may be almost as interesting and controversial as I am.

You have learned a great deal about the Middle Ages and about how your country is governed today. This is important. You do not want someone else making all the important decisions about your life without you having a say or a vote in what happens.

Even if you decided that I was a bad king I don't think I'll bear you a grudge… at the very least, I won't have your head chopped off. I suppose you thought for yourself before you made your mind up. One of the best things about history is that you develop your thinking skills and express your own ideas. It's no fun being told what to think all the time.

Now, if you'll excuse me, I need to say my prayers and then I've got a really good book to read!"

# ◆ Glossary

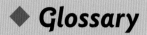

| | |
|---|---|
| ARCHBISHOP OF CANTERBURY | the leader of the Church in England |
| CLERGY | all the people – such as priests, monks and nuns – who have been trained to perform religious duties in the Christian Church and are under the control of the Church courts |
| CRUSADES | the military expeditions led by Christians to recapture the Holy Land from the Muslims during the Middle Ages |
| DEMOCRACY | the government of a country by its people, usually through a parliament elected by the people |
| EXCOMMUNICATION | a punishment given by the Church which ends someone's membership of the Church |
| FREEMAN | a peasant who had achieved some freedom from his lord |
| HUNDRED YEARS WAR | a series of wars in the fourteenth, fifteenth and early sixteenth centuries between England and France, which formed part of a longer conflict that began with the Norman Conquest of England in 1066 |
| INTERDICT | a punishment given by the Church which allows someone to remain a member of the Church, but stops them taking part in certain religious acts (see EXCOMMUNICATION) |
| PAUPER | a very poor person |
| PEASANT | a poor person who worked on the land. The majority of people in medieval England were peasants |
| PREJUDICE | an unreasonable dislike of someone or something, formed without knowledge or experience |
| SUFFRAGETTE | a woman who fought for suffrage, which is the right to vote in political elections |

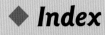

# Index

## ◆ *Titles in the series:*

Pupils' Books are available for all titles.

Teacher's Resource Books are available online at www.hoddereducation.co.uk/thisishistory

## ◆ *Acknowledgements*

The Publishers would like to thank the following for permission to reproduce copyright material:

**Pictures:**
**Cover:** British Library, London, UK; **p.2** Disney Enterprises, Inc.; **p.3** *cl & b* British Library, London, UK/Bridgeman Art Library, *cr* Mary Evans Picture Library; **p.11** British Library, London, UK/Bridgeman Art Library; **p.17** *both* Bridgeman Art Library; **p18** English Heritage Photo Library; **p.19** *l* Bridgeman Art Library, *r* Mary Evans Picture Library; **p.24** *l* from *Kings and Queens of Britain* by J. Ross published by Weidenfeld & Nicolson, *r* with kind permission of Master and Fellows of Corpus Christi College, Cambridge; **p.28** Public Record Office Image Library; **p.30** *both* Bridgeman Art Library; **p.31** *tl* Public Record Office Image Library, *tc & bl* Mary Evans Picture Library, *tr* Bridgeman Art Library, *br* Robert Harding Picture Library; **p.43** *t* Bridgeman Art Library, *c* Weidenfeld (Publishers) Ltd Archive, *bl* Hulton Getty, *br* PA News Photo Library; **p.45** *both* Public Record Office Image Library; **p.54** *cl, bl, bc & br* Bridgeman Art Library, *c & cr* Mary Evans Picture Library; **p.56** Collections; **p.57** *t* Collections, *c* Ffotograff, *b* Bridgeman Art Library; **p.59** *t* Bridgeman Art Library, *b* Ronald Grant Archive; **p.61** *both* Ronald Grant Archive

**Written sources:**
**p.15** *Source 2* W.L. Warren, *King John*, Yale University Press, 1961, *Source 3* R.V. Turner, *King John*, Longman, 1994; **p.34** *Source 5* R. Kipling & C.R.L Fletcher, *A History of England*, Oxford at the Clarendon Press, London, Henry Frowde and Hodder and Stoughton, 1911. By permission of A.P. Watt Ltd on behalf of The National Trust for Places of Historic Interest or Natural Beauty; **p.35** *Source 6* W.L. Warren, *King John*, Yale University Press, 1961

(*t* = top, *b* = bottom, *l* = left, *r* = right, *c* = centre)

Every effort has been made to trace all copyright holders, but if any have been inadvertently overlooked the Publishers will be pleased to make the necessary arrangements at the first opportunity.